Canadian Daily Phonics
Grade 3

About this book:
These 31 weekly lessons teach and review many phonetic and word study concepts needed to develop strong reading, writing, and spelling skills. The lessons cover initial and final consonants; single vowels and vowel combinations; blends and digraphs in the initial and final positions; singular and plural words; syllabication; antonyms, homonyms and synonyms.

Written by Ruth Solski
Illustrated by On The Mark Press

About the author:
Ruth Solski has been an educator for over 30 years and is the founder of S&S Learning Materials, now On The Mark Press. As a writer, she strives to provide teachers with a useful tool to bring the joy of learning to many children. She strongly believes practise makes perfection.

Copyright © On The Mark Press 2017

This publication may be reproduced under licence from Access Copyright, or with the express written permission of On The Mark Press, or as permitted by law. All rights are otherwise reserved, and no part of this publication may be reproduced, stored in a retrieval system, or transmitted in any form or by any means, electronic, mechanical, photocopying, scanning, recording or otherwise, except as specifically authorized.

All Rights Reserved.

Printed in Canada.

Published in Canada by:
On The Mark Press
Belleville, ON
www.onthemarkpress.com

Funded by the Government of Canada

SSR1142 ISBN: 9781771586887

Canadian Daily Phonics

Grade Three

Table of Contents

Sequential Development of Skills..........4	Students Worksheets 6
How to Use This Book.........................5	Weekly Tests 6
Weekly Planning Sheets......................5	Ways to Use the Weekly Plans..............7

Week 1: Alphabetical Ordering 8

Week 2: Initial, Medial and Final Consonants.. 14

Week 3: Recognition of Hard and Soft Cc and Gg.. 20

Week 4: Recognition of the Short Vowel Sounds 'a, u, i'... 26

Week 5: Recognition of Short Vowels 'o' and 'e'... 32

Week 6: Long and Short Vowel Review 38

Week 7: 'Yy' as a Vowel and as a Consonant.. 44

Week 8: 'R' Controlled Vowels: 'ar, er, ir, or, ur'... 50

Week 9: Syllables in Words 56

Week 10: 'R' Blends, 'L' Blends, 'S' Blends... 62

Week 11: Recognition of 'ar, or, ir, ur, er' in Words.. 68

Week 12: Suffixes 'ed, ing, es, er, est' 74

Week 13: Suffixes 'ed, ing, er, est, ly, ness, ful, less' 80

Week 14: Adding Suffixes to Root Words... 86

Week 15: Adding Suffixes 'es' to Words Ending With 'ss, x, ch, sh, f, fe' 92

Week 16: Syllabication 98

Week 17: Regular Double Vowels 'ea, ee, ai, oa, ie, ay, ow'................................... 104

Week 18: Vowel Digraphs 'oo, ea, au, ae, ei' 110

Week 19: Diphthongs 'oi, oy, ou, ow, ew' 116

Week 20: Syllabication 122

Week 21: Consonant Digraphs 'sh, ch, wh, th, ck, kn, ph, gn, wr, gh' 128

Week 22: Recognition of Prefixes 134

Week 23: Prefixes, Root Words, Suffixes 140

Week 24: Syllabication Rules 1 to 5 146

Week 25: Syllabication Rules 6 and 7 152

Week 26: Syllabication Rules 8, 9, and 10 158

Week 27: Review of Syllabication Rules 1 to 10 164

Week 28: Recognition of Contractions 170

Week 29: Recognizing and Using Antontyms 176

Week 30: Recognizing and Using Homonyms 182

Week 31: Recognizing and Using Synonyms 188

Phonics Information for Teachers and Parents 194

Development and Progress Chart for a Student's Phonetic Skills 199

Student Phonics Award 200

Canadian Daily Phonics
Sequential Development of Skills

Week 1: Review the Formation and Ordering of the Letters of the Alphabet.
Week 2: Recognition of Initial, Medial and Final Consonants
Week 3: Recognition of Hard and Soft 'C' and 'G'
Week 4: Recognition of Short Vowel Sounds 'a, u, and i'
Week 5: Recognition of Short Vowels 'o' and 'e'
Week 6: Long and Short Vowel Review
Week 7: Recognition of 'Yy' as a vowel and as a Consonant
Week 8: Recognition of 'ar, er, ir, or, ur' in Words
Week 9: Recognition of Syllables in Words
Week 10: Recognition and Usage of 'R, L, and S' Blends
Week 11: Recognition of 'ar, or, ir, ur, and er' in Words
Week 12: Using Suffixes 'ed, ing, es, er, est' in Words
Week 13: Suffix Rules for Adding 'ed, ing, er, est, ly, ness, ful, less'
Week 14: Adding Suffixes to Root Words
Week 15: Adding the Suffixes to Words Ending With 'ss, x, ch, sh, f, fe'
Week 16: Recognizing Syllables in Words
Week 17: Regular Double Vowels 'ea, ee, oi, oa, ie, ay, ow'
Week 18: Vowel Digraphs 'oo, ea, au, ee, ei'
Week 19: Diphthongs 'oi, oy, ou, ow, ew'
Week 20: Syllabication in Words With Regular and Irregular Double Vowels
Week 21: Consonant Digraphs 'sh, ch, wh, th, ck, kn, ph, gn, wr, gh'
Week 22: Recognition of Prefixes 'un, dis, ex, de, re'
Week 23: Prefixes, Root Words, Suffixes
Week 24: Syllabication Rules 1 to 5
Week 25: Syllabication Rules 6 to 7
Week 26: Syllabication Rules 8, 9, 10
Week 27: Review of Syllabication Rules One to Ten
Week 28: Recognition of Contractions
Week 29: Recognition of Antonyms
Week 30: Recognition of Homonyms

How to Use This Book

The Canadian Phonics Book for Grade Three contains thirty-one weekly lesson plans for the various phonetic skills required by Grade Three students to help develop their reading, writing and spelling skills. Each week contains a Lesson Plan for each day, Daily Worksheets, Identification for pictures used, Answer Keys for Daily Worksheets and a Weekly Test.

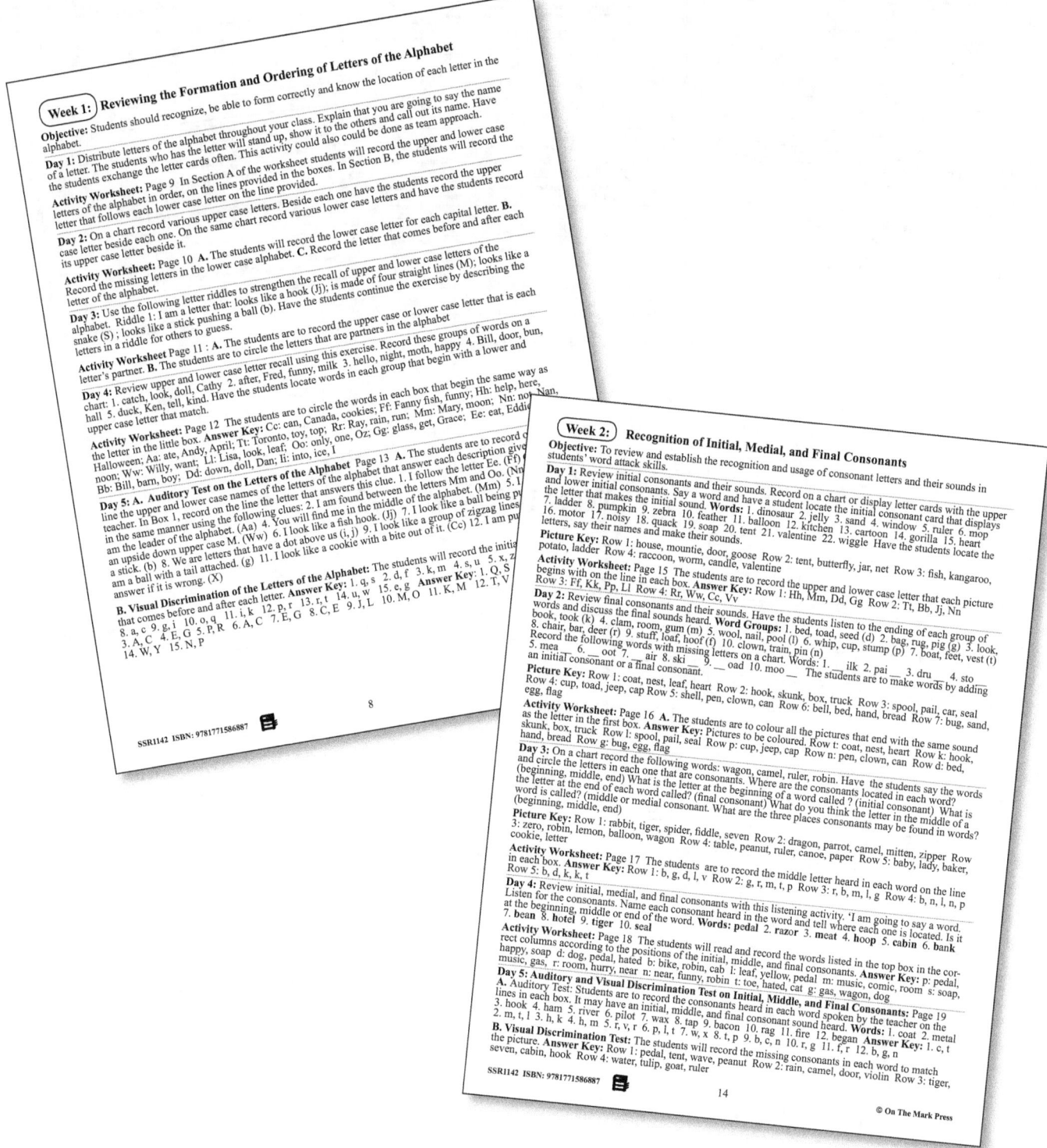

Student Worksheets

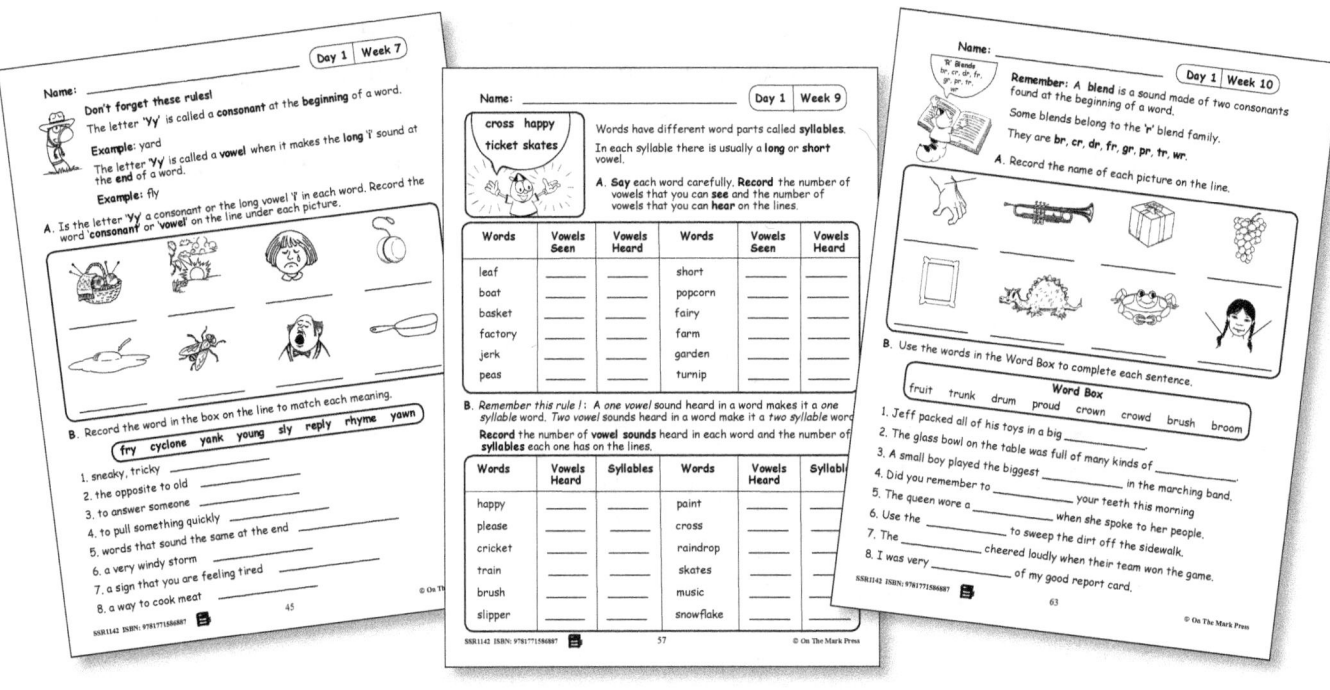

Weekly Tests

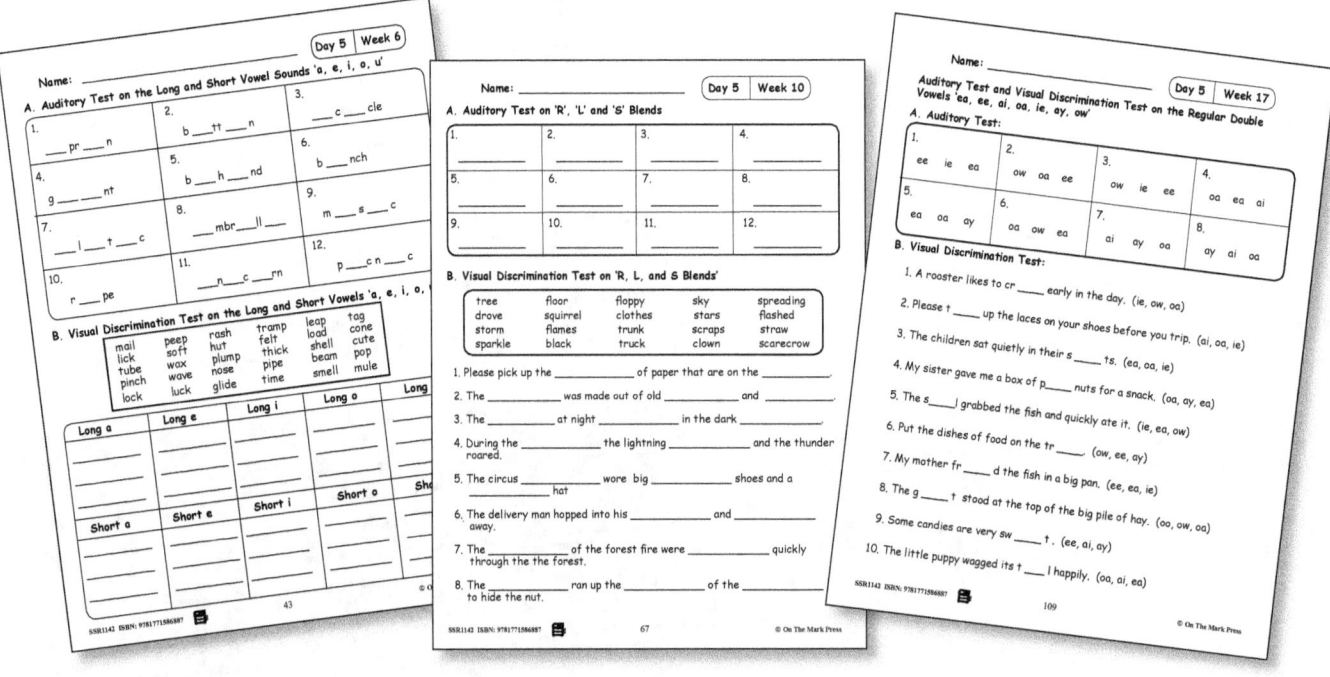

Ways to Use the Weekly Lesson Plans and Weekly Activities

The teaching plans and activity sheets could be used with students in the following ways:

- on a weekly basis with a class or group of students

or

- the ideas and worksheets could be used to suit students' needs

or

- they could be used for teaching ideas

or

- to reinforce individual students' phonetic skills during home study.

Each weekly plan contains an:

- Objective

- Teacher Information

- Daily Planning Ideas containing games, listening activities, stories and riddles.

- A Picture Key is provided for each worksheet that has pictures so they can be identified.

- Four Weekly Activity Worksheets focus on the concept(s) taught during the week.

- Weekly Tests are provided and could be held on the last day of the week or when it is necessary.

Week 1: Reviewing the Formation and Ordering of Letters of the Alphabet

Objective: Students should recognize, be able to form correctly and know the location of each letter in the alphabet.

Day 1: Distribute letters of the alphabet throughout your class. Explain that you are going to say the name of a letter. The students who has the letter will stand up, show it to the others and call out its name. Have the students exchange the letter cards often. This activity could also be done as a team approach.

Activity Worksheet: Page 9 In Section A of the worksheet students will record the upper and lower case letters of the alphabet in order, on the lines provided in the boxes. In Section B, the students will record the letter that follows each lower case letter on the line provided.

Day 2: On a chart record various upper case letters. Beside each one have the students record the upper case letter beside each one. On the same chart record various lower case letters and have the students record its upper case letter beside it.

Activity Worksheet: Page 10 **A.** The students will record the lower case letter for each capital letter. **B.** Record the missing letters in the lower case alphabet. **C.** Record the letter that comes before and after each letter of the alphabet.

Day 3: A. Use the following letter riddles to strengthen the recall of upper and lower case letters of the alphabet. Riddle 1: I am a letter that: looks like a hook (Jj); is made of four straight lines (M); looks like a snake (S); looks like a stick pushing a ball **B.** Have the students continue the exercise by describing the letters in a riddle for others to guess.

Activity Worksheet Page 11 **A.** The students are to record the upper case or lower case letter that is each letter's partner. **B.** The students are to circle the letters that are partners in the alphabet

Day 4: Review upper and lower case letter recall using this exercise. Record these groups of words on a chart: 1. catch, look, doll, Cathy 2. after, Fred, funny, milk 3. hello, night, moth, happy 4. Bill, door, bun, hall 5. duck, Ken, tell, kind. Have the students locate words in each group that begin with a lower and upper case letter that match.

Activity Worksheet: Page 12 The students are to circle the words in each box that begin the same way as the letter in the little box. **Answer Key:** Cc: can, Canada, cookies; Ff: Fanny fish, funny; Hh: help, here, Halloween; Aa: ate, Andy, April; Tt: Toronto, toy, top; Rr: Ray, rain, run; Mm: Mary, moon; Nn: not, Nan, noon; Ww: Willy, want; Ll: Lisa, look, leaf; Oo: only, one, Oz; Gg: glass, get, Grace; Ee: eat, Eddie; Bb: Bill, barn, boy; Dd: down, doll, Dan; Ii: into, ice, I

Day 5: A. Auditory Test on the Letters of the Alphabet Page 13 **A.** The students are to record on the line the upper and lower case names of the letters of the alphabet that answer each description given by the teacher. In Box 1, record on the line the letter that answers this clue. 1. I follow the letter Ee. (Ff) Continue in the same manner using the following clues: 2. I am found between the letters Mm and Oo. (Nn) 3. I am the leader of the alphabet. (Aa) 4. You will find me in the middle of the alphabet. (Mm) 5. I look like an upside down upper case M. (Ww) 6. I look like a fish hook. (Jj) 7. I look like a ball being pushed by a stick. (b) 8. We are letters that have a dot above us (i, j) 9. I look like a group of zigzag lines. (z) 10. I am a ball with a tail attached. (g) 11. I look like a cookie with a bite out of it. (Cc) 12. I am put beside an answer if it is wrong. (X)

B. Visual Discrimination of the Letters of the Alphabet: The students will record the initial consonant that comes before and after each letter. **Answer Key:** 1. q, s 2. d, f 3. k, m 4. s, u 5. x, z 6. f, h 7. l, n 8. a, c 9. g, i 10. o, q 11. i, k 12. p, r 13. r, t 14. u, w 15. e, g **Answer Key:** 1. Q, S 2. L, N 3. A, C 4. E, G 5. P, R 6. A, C 7. E, G 8. C, E 9. J, L 10. M, O 11. K, M 12. T, V 13. V, X 14. W, Y 15. N, P

Name: _____   Day 1 | Week 1

How well do you know the letters found in the alphabet?

Did you know that capital letters are called upper case letters and their partners are called lower case letters?

Examples: Aa, Bb, Cc, Dd

A. Write the upper case and lower case letters of the alphabet on the lines in each box.

B. Write the letter that follows each letter in the alphabet.

p ____   q ____   n ____   d ____

x ____   t ____   p ____   h ____

d ____   c ____   r ____   y ____

y ____   w ____   x ____   i ____

a ____   o ____   s ____   a ____

Name: _____ Day 2 | Week 1

How well do you know the letters in the alphabet?
Can you print them in the correct order?

A. Print each letter's partner on the line in each box.

🍎	C ___	A ___	G ___	M ___	O ___	🥁
B ___	H ___	D ___	J ___	T ___	V ___	W ___
N ___	S ___	R ___	U ___	Y ___	Z ___	I ___
X ___	E ___	K ___	F ___	L ___	P ___	Q ___

B. Print the small letters that are missing from the alphabet.

a ___ ___ d ___ f g ___ i j k ___

___ ___ ___ p ___ r s ___ u v

___ x ___ ___

C. Print the upper case letter for each lower case letter.

___ j	___ q	___ z	___ x	___ l	___ v	___ g
___ c	___ s	___ n	___ o	___ w	___ y	___ p

10

Name: _____ | Day 3 | Week 1 |

Each letter of the alphabet has a partner.
Each pair has an upper case letter with a lower case partner.

A. Record each letter's partner on the line beside it.

A ____	B ____	a ____	j ____
s ____	D ____	O ____	E ____
z ____	F ____	C ____	R ____
K ____	J ____	E ____	B ____
t ____	R ____	y ____	Q ____
m ____	G ____	X ____	M ____
i ____	L ____	t ____	H ____
l ____	P ____	N ____	C ____
n ____	Q ____	u ____	S ____
K ____	I ____	V ____	K ____

B. Circle the letters that are partners in the alphabet.

B d	R r	L t	N n	E e	P q
H q	M n	N m	P p	U v	W y
S s	F g	Z z	O c	W v	X x

Name: _____   Day 4 | Week 1

How well do you know the letters of the alphabet?

Circle the words in the big box that begin the same way as the letters in the little box.

C c	doll	can	much	Canada	cookies
F f	off	Fanny	gift	fish	funny
H h	help	night	day	here	Halloween
A a	Andy	ate	pull	dog	April
T t	Help	Toronto	toy	home	top
R r	barn	Ray	rain	here	run
M m	come	nap	Mary	some	moon
N n	may	not	Nan	run	noon
W w	cow	Willy	want	away	new
L l	Lisa	all	look	ball	leaf
O o	boat	only	four	one	Oz
G g	bag	glass	get	Grace	log
E e	eat	Eddie	sat	need	dime
B b	Bill	barn	boy	door	pig
D d	down	ball	doll	find	Dan
I i	into	ice	I	went	find

SSR1142 ISBN: 9781771586887   12   © On The Mark Press

Name: _____ Day 5 | Week 1

A. Auditory Test on the Letters of the Alphabet

| 1. ____ | 2. ____ | 3. ____ | 4. ____ | 5. ____ | 6. ____ |
| 7. ____ | 8. ____ | 9. ____ | 10. ____ | 11. ____ | 12. ____ |

B. Visual Discrimination of the letters of the Alphabet

1. Record the **lower** case letters that come **before** and **after** each member of the alphabet.

1. ____ r ____	6. ____ g ____	11. ____ j ____
2. ____ e ____	7. ____ m ____	12. ____ q ____
3. ____ l ____	8. ____ b ____	13. ____ s ____
4. ____ t ____	9. ____ h ____	14. ____ v ____
5. ____ y ____	10. ____ p ____	15. ____ f ____

2. Record the **upper** case letters that come **before** and **after** each member of the alphabet.

1. ____ R ____	6. ____ B ____	11. ____ L ____
2. ____ M ____	7. ____ F ____	12. ____ U ____
3. ____ B ____	8. ____ D ____	13. ____ W ____
4. ____ F ____	9. ____ K ____	14. ____ X ____
5. ____ Q ____	10. ____ N ____	15. ____ O ____

Week 2: Recognition of Initial, Medial, and Final Consonants

Objective: To review and establish the recognition and usage of consonant letters and their sounds in students' word attack skills.

Day 1: Review initial consonants and their sounds. Record on a chart or display letter cards with the upper and lower initial consonants. Say a word and have a student locate the initial consonant card that displays the letter that makes the initial sound. **Words:** 1. dinosaur 2. jelly 3. sand 4. window 5. ruler 6. mop 7. ladder 8. pumpkin 9. zebra 10. feather 11. balloon 12. kitchen 13. cartoon 14. gorilla 15. heart 16. motor 17. noisy 18. quack 19. soap 20. tent 21. valentine 22. wiggle Have the students locate the letters, say their names and make their sounds.

Picture Key: Row 1: house, mountie, door, goose Row 2: tent, butterfly, jar, net Row 3: fish, kangaroo, potato, ladder Row 4: raccoon, worm, candle, valentine

Activity Worksheet: Page 15 The students are to record the upper and lower case letter that each picture begins with on the line in each box. **Answer Key:** Row 1: Hh, Mm, Dd, Gg Row 2: Tt, Bb, Jj, Nn Row 3: Ff, Kk, Pp, Ll Row 4: Rr, Ww, Cc, Vv

Day 2: Review final consonants and their sounds. Have the students listen to the ending of each group of words and discuss the final sounds heard. **Word Groups:** 1. bed, toad, seed (d) 2. bag, rug, pig (g) 3. look, book, took (k) 4. clam, room, gum (m) 5. wool, nail, pool (l) 6. whip, cup, stump (p) 7. boat, feet, vest (t) 8. chair, bar, deer (r) 9. stuff, loaf, hoof (f) 10. clown, train, pin (n)
Record the following words with missing letters on a chart. Words: 1. __ ilk 2. pai __ 3. dru __ 4. sto __ 5. mea __ 6. __ oot 7. __ air 8. ski __ 9. __ oad 10. moo __   The students are to make words by adding an initial consonant or a final consonant.

Picture Key: Row 1: coat, nest, leaf, heart Row 2: hook, skunk, box, truck Row 3: spool, pail, car, seal Row 4: cup, toad, jeep, cap Row 5: shell, pen, clown, can Row 6: bell, bed, hand, bread Row 7: bug, sand, egg, flag

Activity Worksheet: Page 16 **A.** The students are to colour all the pictures that end with the same sound as the letter in the first box. **Answer Key:** Pictures to be coloured. Row t: coat, nest, heart Row k: hook, skunk, box, truck Row l: spool, pail, seal Row p: cup, jeep, cap Row n: pen, clown, can Row d: bed, hand, bread Row g: bug, egg, flag

Day 3: On a chart record the following words: wagon, camel, ruler, robin. Have the students say the words and circle the letters in each one that are consonants. Where are the consonants located in each word? (beginning, middle, end) What is the letter at the beginning of a word called? (initial consonant) What is the letter at the end of each word called? (final consonant) What do you think the letter in the middle of a word is called? (middle or medial consonant. What are the three places consonants may be found in words? (beginning, middle, end)

Picture Key: Row 1: rabbit, tiger, spider, fiddle, seven Row 2: dragon, parrot, camel, mitten, zipper Row 3: zero, robin, lemon, balloon, wagon Row 4: table, peanut, ruler, canoe, paper Row 5: baby, lady, baker, cookie, letter

Activity Worksheet: Page 17 The students are to record the middle letter heard in each word on the line in each box. **Answer Key:** Row 1: b, g, d, l, v Row 2: g, r, m, t, p Row 3: r, b, m, l, g Row 4: b, n, l, n, p Row 5: b, d, k, k, t

Day 4: Review initial, medial, and final consonants with this listening activity. 'I am going to say a word. Listen for the consonants. Name each consonant heard in the word and tell where each one is located. Is it at the beginning, middle or end of the word. **Words: pedal** 2. **razor** 3. **meat** 4. **hoop** 5. **cabin** 6. **bank** 7. **bean** 8. **hotel** 9. **tiger** 10. **seal**

Activity Worksheet: Page 18 The students will read and record the words listed in the top box in the correct columns according to the positions of the initial, middle, and final consonants. **Answer Key:** p: pedal, happy, soap d: dog, pedal, hated b: bike, robin, cab l: leaf, yellow, pedal m: music, comic, room s: soap, music, gas, r: room, hurry, near n: near, funny, robin t: toe, hated, cat g: gas, wagon, dog

Day 5: Auditory and Visual Discrimination Test on Initial, Middle, and Final Consonants: Page 19 **A.** Auditory Test: Students are to record the consonants heard in each word spoken by the teacher on the lines in each box. It may have an initial, middle, and final consonant sound heard. **Words:** 1. coat 2. metal 3. hook 4. ham 5. river 6. pilot 7. wax 8. tap 9. bacon 10. rag 11. fire 12. began **Answer Key:** 1. c, t 2. m, t, l 3. h, k 4. h, m 5. r, v, r 6. p, l, t 7. w, x 8. t, p 9. b, c, n 10. r, g 11. f, r 12. b, g, n

B. Visual Discrimination Test: The students will record the missing consonants in each word to match the picture. **Answer Key:** Row 1: pedal, tent, wave, peanut Row 2: rain, camel, door, violin Row 3: tiger, seven, cabin, hook Row 4: water, tulip, goat, ruler

Name: _____   Day 1 | Week 2

How well do you know the initial consonants and their sounds?

They often begin words.

Record the upper and lower case letter that makes the beginning sound of each picture on the line beneath it.

Initial consonants are important letters in words!

      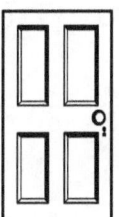   

____   ____   ____   ____

____   ____   ____   ____

      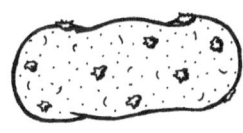   

____   ____   ____   ____

   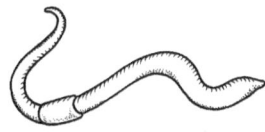      

____   ____   ____   ____

Name: _____ Day 2 | Week 2

Watch the ends of words!

Most words end with a **final consonant**.

Examples: coa**t**, bo**x**, lam**p**, hil**l**, han**d**, ca**p**

Say the name of each picture. **Colour** all the pictures in each row that end with the **same sound** made by the letter in the first box.

t	coat	nest	leaf	heart
k	hook	skunk	box	truck
l	spool	pail	car	seal
p	cup	frog	jeep	cap
n	shell	pen	clown	can
d	bell	bed	hand	bread
g	bug	sand	egg	flag

Name: _____ Day 3 | Week 2

 Always look for consonants inside words.

Did you know that some consonants are found in the **middle** of words.

Examples: broken   tulip   cabin

Record on the line, in each box, the consonant heard in the middle of each picture.

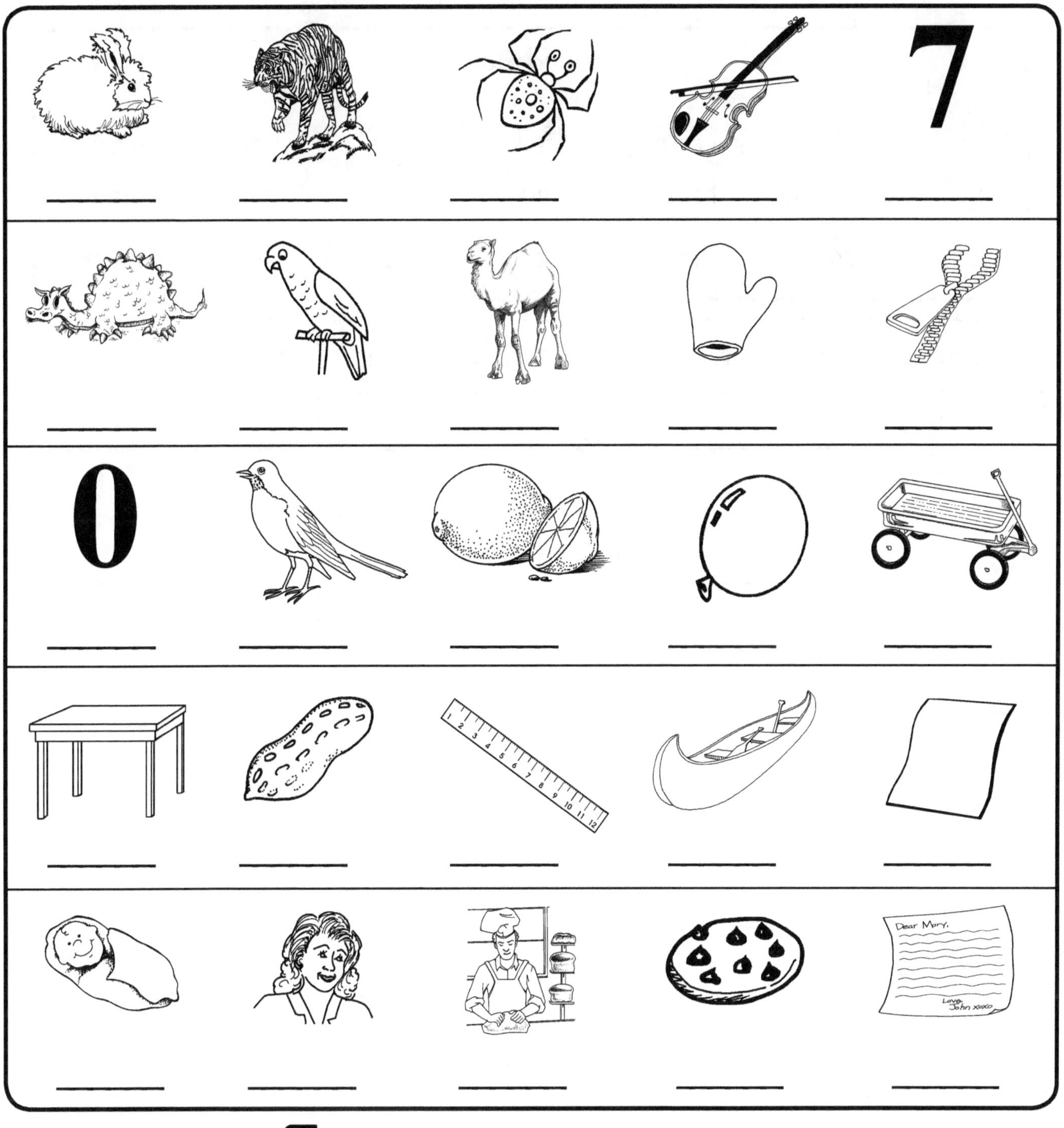

Name: _____ Day 4 | Week 2

Remember **consonants** are letters of the alphabet that can be found at the **beginning**, in the **middle** or at the **end** of words.

Consonants may be found in many places in words.

Record the words in the Word Box that tells where the letter is found in the correct column.

Word Box						
music	bike	pedal	leaf	soap	hated	comic
dog	yellow	toe	cab	robin	hurry	near
room	cat	gas	near	happy	funny	wagon

Letter	Beginning Consonant	Middle Consonant	Ending Consonant
p	_____	_____	_____
d	_____	_____	_____
b	_____	_____	_____
l	_____	_____	_____
m	_____	_____	_____
s	_____	_____	_____
r	_____	_____	_____
n	_____	_____	_____
t	_____	_____	_____
g	_____	_____	_____

Name: _____   Day 5 | Week 2

A. Auditory Test of the Initial, Middle, and Final Consonants

1. __ __ __	2. __ __ __	3. __ __ __	4. __ __ __
5. __ __ __	6. __ __ __	7. __ __ __	8. __ __ __
9. __ __ __	10. __ __ __	11. __ __ __	12. __ __ __

B. Visual Discrimination Test of Initial, Middle, and Final Consonants

__e__a__	__en__	__a__e__	__ea__u__
__ai__	__a__e__	__oo__	__io__i__
__i__e__	__e__e__	__a__i__	__oo__
__a__e__	__u__i__	__oa__	__u__e__

Week 3: Recognition of Hard and Soft C and G

Objective: To make students aware that the initial consonants 'Cc' and 'Gg' have a hard and a soft sound.

Day 1: On a chart record the following groups of words: **Group 1** - candy, cat, cookie, corn **Group 2:** cent, celery, cereal, city. Have the students say each group of words. What letter is at the beginning of each word in each group. (Cc) What sound does each word in Group 1 begin with? (cuh) What sound do you hear at the beginning of the words in the second group? (the sound that 's' makes) Explain to your students that the consonant 'Cc' is able to make two sounds. It has a 'hard Cc' sound and a 'soft Cc' sound. The hard 'Cc' is usually heard at the beginning or inside words and sometimes at the end of a word. Examples: coat, cactus, become, arc. The soft 'Cc' sound is in 'cent, face, ice, cereal.' It is found at the beginning and in the middle of a word.

Picture Key: Row 1: cent, candle Row 2: camel, face Row 3: pencil, circle Row 4: can, fence, Row 5: mice, candy

Activity Worksheet: Page 21 The students will record the name of the sound and where it is located in the picture. **Answer Key:** 1. Soft C; beginning 2. Hard C; beginning 3. Hard C; beginning 4. Soft C; middle 5. Soft C; middle 6. Soft C, Hard C; beginning, middle 7. Hard C; beginning 8. Soft C; middle 9. Soft C; middle 10. Hard C; beginning

Day 2: Review the hard and soft sounds made by the consonant 'Cc.' Record the following words on a chart: cage, cell, face, black, cave, dancer, recess, circus, cold, prince. Have the students circle the words with the hard 'Cc' sound and underline the words with the soft 'Cc' sound. Remind them that when 'c' is followed by an 'e' or a 'y', the 'c' is usually soft. The soft 'c' makes the sound that 's' stands for as well.

Activity Worksheet: Page 22 The students will classify the words that have a hard or soft 'c' on a chart. **Answer Key:** *Candy* - cows, crib, cape, coach, cake, cane, cave, cap, doctor, cookies *Pencil* - recess, grace, dance, excited, price, race, mice, place, cellar, fence

Day 3: Introduce the Hard and Soft Gg using these sentences: 1. George was a gentle gorilla who lived in a large cage at a zoo beside Gus the tall giraffe. 2. The big dog began to bark at the huge guy who was walking in the garden. Underline the designated words. Have the students read the sentences. What is the same letter seen in the underlined words. (Gg) Does the 'Gg' make the same sound in each word? (no) What sound does it make? (It makes the same sound as the letter 'j' and the letter 'g.' Explain that the letter 'Gg' has a hard and soft sound. Its hard sound is 'guh' and its soft sound is 'juh.' The hard and soft Gg can be heard at the beginning, in the middle and at the end of a word.

Picture Key: 1. cage 2. game 3. girl 4. orange 5. bridge 6. wagon 7. stage 8. vegetables 9. frog 10. gift

Activity Worksheet: Page 23 The students will record the name of the sound and its location in each word. **Answer Key:** 1. soft g; end 2. hard g; beginning 3. hard g; beginning 4. soft g; end 5. soft g; end 6. hard g; middle 7. soft g; end 8. soft g; middle 9. hard g; end 10. hard g; beginning

Day 4: Review the Hard and Soft 'Cc' and 'Gg' with the following riddles: 1. I am a kind of hat that begins with a hard c. (cap) 2. I am sweet to chew and begin with a hard 'g.' (gum) 3. It is a home for a car and begins with a hard 'g' and ends with a a soft 'g.' (garage) 4. I am a home for a pet bird. A soft 'g' is found inside me. (cage) 5. It is a place where plants grow. It begins with a hard 'g.' (garden) 6. We travel through the air and on things. We make people sick. Our name begins with the soft 'g.' (germs) 7. I end with a soft 'g.' I am something that you put on a cut. (bandage) 8. I begin with a soft 'g' and have a soft 'g' inside me. I am a kind of spice. (ginger) 9. This is something taken away from buildings every week. It begins with a hard 'g' and ends with a soft 'g.' (garbage) 10. I am a little farm animal with horns. My name begins with a hard 'g' sound. (goat)

Activity Worksheet: Page 24 The students will classify the words in the Word Box under the correct heading. **Answer Key:** Hard C - cattle, candy, doctor, cookies, corn, Soft C - price, palace, cement, recess, decide Hard G - game, flag, ugly, garden, sugar Soft G - page, engine, orange, large, giant

Day 5: Auditory Test on the Hard and Soft Cc and Gg: Page 25 The students are to print the name of the sound heard in each word said by the teacher. **Words:** 1. rice 2. guard 3. garage 4. coach 5. circus 6. grant 7. cereal 8. hug **Answer Key:** 1. soft c 2. hard g 3. hard g, soft g 4. hard c 5. soft c, hard c 6. hard g 7. soft c 8. hard g

B. Visual Discrimination Test on the Hard and Soft Cc and Gg: The students are to record the name of the letter 'c' or 'g' that is heard in each word. **Answer Key:** 1. Hard c 2. Soft g 3. Hard g 4. Hard c 5. Hard g 6. Soft c 7. Soft g 8. Soft c 9. Hard c 10. Soft c 11. Soft g 12. Soft c 13. Hard c 14. Hard c 15. Soft g 16. Hard g 17. Soft c 18. Soft g 19. Hard Gg 20. Soft g

Name: _____   Day 1 | Week 3

The consonant 'Cc' makes two sounds.

It has a **hard** sound as in 'cake' and a 'soft' sound as in the word 'cent'. Both sounds may be heard at the **beginning** of a word or in the **middle** of one.

Examples: Hard 'Cc' - cat, picture   Soft 'Cc' - cereal, face

On the lines in each box **record** the **name** of the sound that 'Cc' makes and **where** it is found in the word.

1. Sound: _____ Location: _____	2. Sound: _____ Location: _____
3. Sound: _____ Location: _____	4. Sound: _____ Location: _____
5. Sound: _____ Location: _____	6. Sound: _____ Location: _____
7. Sound: _____ Location: _____	8. Sound: _____ Location: _____
9. Sound: _____ Location: _____	10. Sound: _____ Location: _____

Name: _____   Day 2 | Week 3

Read this helpful tip! 
Remember: When the letter 'c' is followed by the letters 'e, or i, the 'c' is usually **soft**. The **soft** 'c' stands for the sound that 's' makes.

Record the words in the box that contain the **hard** 'c' sound under the picture of **candy** and the **soft** 'c' words under the picture of a **pencil**.

recess	cape	coach	mice	doctor
cows	dance	cake	cave	cookies
grace	excited	race	place	cellar
crib	price	cane	cap	fence

candy

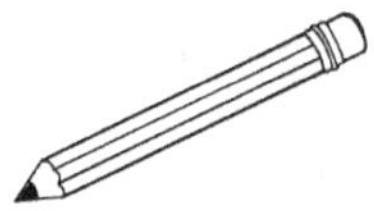

_____
_____
_____
_____
_____
_____
_____
_____

pencil

_____
_____
_____
_____
_____
_____
_____
_____

Name: _____ Day 3 | Week 3

Did you know that the consonant '**Gg**' has a **soft** sound and a **hard** sound?

It has a **hard** sound as in '**gate**' and a **soft** sound as in '**giant**.'

Both sounds may be heard at the **beginning**, in the **middle** or at the **end** of a word.

Examples: Hard 'Gg' - good, again, dog   Soft 'Gg' - giant, danger, page

On the line in each box **record** the name of the sound and where it is found.

1. Sound: _____ Location: _____	2. Sound: _____ Location: _____
3. Sound: _____ Location: _____	4. Sound: _____ Location: _____
5. Sound: _____ Location: _____	6. Sound: _____ Location: _____
7. Sound: _____ Location: _____	8. Sound: _____ Location: _____
9. Sound: _____ Location: _____	10. Sound: _____ Location: _____

Name: _____   Day 4 | Week 3

Here are **two** rules to remember about the **Hard** and **Soft** '**Cc**' and '**Gg**.'

Rule 1: When **Cc** is followed by **e, i,** or **y,** the **c** is usually **soft**. The soft 'c' stands for the sound that 's' makes.

Rule 2: When **Gg** is followed by **e, i,** or **y,** the **Gg** usually has a **soft** sound. The **soft Gg** stands for the sound that the letter '**j**' makes.

Record each word in the Word Box under the correct heading.

cattle	flag	cement	ugly	giant
game	palace	orange	garden	decide
page	engine	doctor	cookies	large
price	candy	recess	sugar	corn

Hard Cc

_____
_____
_____
_____
_____

Hard Gg

_____
_____
_____
_____
_____

Soft Cc

_____
_____
_____
_____
_____

Soft Gg

_____
_____
_____
_____
_____

Name: _____   Day 5 | Week 3

A. Auditory Test on the Hard and Soft 'Cc' and 'Gg'

1. Hard ____ Soft ____	2. Hard ____ Soft ____	3. Hard ____ Soft ____	4. Hard ____ Soft ____
5. Hard ____ Soft ____	6. Hard ____ Soft ____	7. Hard ____ Soft ____	8. Hard ____ Soft ____

B. Visual Discrimination Test on the Hard and Soft 'Cc' and 'Gg'

Is the 'c' or 'g' in each word **hard or soft**?

1. corn _____
2. bridge _____
3. good _____
4. music _____
5. gown _____
6. city _____
7. gentle _____
8. princess _____
9. cork _____
10. pencil _____

11. page _____
12. prance _____
13. canon _____
14. kick _____
15. strange _____
16. game _____
17. fancy _____
18. danger _____
19. flag _____
20. huge _____

Week 4: Recognition of Short Vowel Sounds 'a, u, and i'

Objective: To develop a strong recognition of the sounds made by the short vowels 'a, u, i' and their usage in developing strong word attack skills.

Day 1: Record the following sentence on a chart: Cassie Cat ran after a fat, black rat across the grass in the backyard. Have the students read the sentence silently and aloud. What letter appears in most of the words. (the vowel a) What sound does the vowel 'a' say in each one? (Short 'a' sound) What other sound does the vowel 'a' make? (It says its own name.) What type of vowel is it that says its own name? (a long vowel) Play the following listening game. Listen carefully to each word that I say. If the word has the long 'a' sound put up your hand. If the word has a short 'a' sound, put your hand on your head. **Words:** ran, game, chance, shape, mask, clam, tape, face, fat, ape, ax, page

Picture Key: A. - Row 1: cap, cape, hand, plane, clam Row 2: hat, tap, tape, can, cane **B.** - Row 1: fan, moon, axe, hat, mitten Row 2: rose, pan, rope, can, bat Row 3: kite, apple, glass, tent, lamp

Activity Worksheet: Page 27 **A.** The students will spell the name of each picture and record it on the line. Then they are to circle only the words with the short 'a' vowel sound. **B.** The students are to colour only the pictures that have a short 'a' vowel sound. **Answer Key:** A - Row 1: cap, cape, hand, plane, clam Row 2: hat, tap, tape, can, cane **Circled words:** cap, hand, clam, hat, tap, can **B. Pictures to be coloured:** fan, ax, hat, pan, bat, glass, lamp, apple

Day 2: Record the following story on a chart. **Story:** Phil and Jill were two little pink pigs. They lived on a farm in a big pig pen. Their pen was filled with thick, stinky, slippery mud. Phil and Jill liked to slip, slide, and roll in the stinky mud until they became brown pigs. Have the story read silently. Then have the students read it aloud. Ask: What vowel sound do you hear and see in many of the words in the story. (the short vowel i) What is the other sound that the vowel 'i' makes? (It can say its own name.) What type of vowel is it? (long vowel) **Listening Game:** Listen carefully to each word that I say. If the word has a short vowel 'i', clap your hands. If the word has a long vowel 'i', raise one hand. **Words:** stick, wipe, print, rifle, prize, wrist, file, chime, picnic

Picture Key: **A. Row 1:** dish, mice, milk, lips, ice **Row 2:** dime, grin, whip, nine, pin **B. Row 1:** dice, brick, king, whistle, fire **Row 2:** lion, stickman, bike, chicks, fish **Row 3:** slide, bridge, knife, sink, ring

Activity Worksheet: Page 28 **A.** The students are to record on the line the name of each picture and to circle only the words with the short 'i' sound. **B.** The students are to colour only the pictures with the short vowel 'i.' **Answer Key:** dish, mice, milk, lips, ice, dime, grin, whip, nine, pin **Circled Words:** dish, milk, lips, grin, whip, pin **B. Coloured Pictures:** brick, king, whistle, stickman, chicks, fish, bridge, sink, ring

Day 3: Review the short vowel 'u' sound using the poem called 'Trump the Skunk.' Underline the words as indicated. Read the poem with your students. Discuss the underlined words What vowel sound do you hear in each underlined word? (short u vowel) What sound does the short 'u' make in a word. (uh)

Trump the Skunk

In a hole <u>under</u> a big old <u>stump</u>,
Lived a little <u>skunk</u> called <u>Trump</u>.
During the day, <u>Trump</u> would sleep
As <u>snug</u> as a <u>bug</u> in a <u>rug</u> and didn't make a peep.
Late at night, <u>Trump</u> left his <u>bunk</u>
To look for <u>plump</u> <u>bugs</u> and <u>nuts</u> to <u>munch</u>.
But when there was danger <u>lurking</u> about,
<u>Up</u> went his tail, his back feet would <u>thump</u>
And out flew spray that really <u>stunk</u>!

Picture Key: A. Row 1: tube, rug, trunk, flute, tub **Row 2:** jug, bus, ruler, drum, glue **B. Row 1:** mule, duck, drum, puppy, button **Row 2:** pump, glue, thumb, sun, tube **Row 3:** nut, cup, clue, clap, plum

Activity Worksheet: Page 29 **A.** The students are to record on the line the name of each picture and to circle only the words with the short 'u' sound. **B.** The students are to colour only the pictures with the short 'o' sound. **Answer Key: A.** Row 1. tube, rug, trunk, flute, tub Row 2: jug, bus, ruler cube, puck **Circled Words:** Row 1. rug, trunk, tub Row 2: jug, bus, puck **B. Pictures to be coloured:** duck, drum, pup, button, thumb, pump, sun, nut, cup, plum

Day 4: Have the students practise using their word attack skills using the vowel sounds 'a, i, and u.' Explain that many new words can be made by changing the vowel sound inside the word. Look at each group of words. Say them. Which word doesn't belong in each group. Circle it. Tell why. 1. sip, sap, sup 2. run, rin, ran 3. dush, dish, dash 4. dig, dog, dag 5. mud, med, mad 6. dump, lamp, dimp 7. hung, hing, hang

Activity Worksheet: Page 30 The students are to complete each sentence with the correct word. **Answer Key:** 1. fun 2. bag 3. ham 4. lock 5. sank 6. peck 7. bit 8. puck 9. trick 10. mist

Day 5: Auditory and Visual Discrimination Test on the Short Vowel Sounds 'a, i, u': Page 31

A. Auditory Test: The students are to circle the short vowel sound heard in each word spoken by the teacher. **Words:** 1. dish 2. plug 3. twig 4. under 5. lamp 6. milk 7. wax 8. gift 9. stamp 10. fish **Answer Key:** 1. i 2. u 3. i 4. u 5. a 6. i 7. a 8. i 9. a 10. i

B. Visual Discrimination Test: The students will record the correct word from the Word Box in each sentence. **Answer Key:** 1. bridge 2. fist 3. buds 4. quack 5. pump 6. jingle 7. match 8. suds 9. trunk 10. picnic

Name: _____   Day 1 | Week 4

The letter 'a' is a **vowel**. It has a **long** and a **short** sound.

Its **long** sound is the same as its name, and its **short** sound makes the sound heard in '**cat**.'

A. Record the name of each picture. Circle the words that have the same short vowel 'a.'

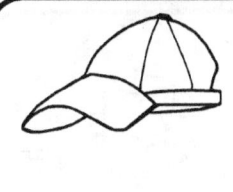 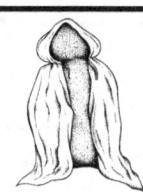 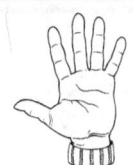  

_____ _____ _____ _____ _____

  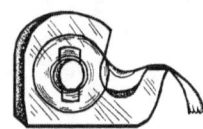  

_____ _____ _____ _____ _____

B. Say the name of each picture. **Colour** the pictures with the short vowel 'a' sound.

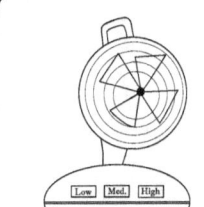 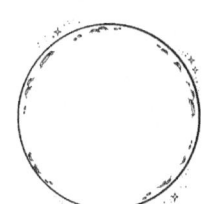   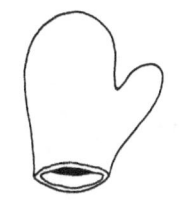

 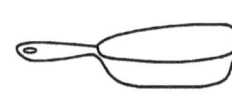   

Name: _____   Day 2 | Week 4

The letter 'i' is a **vowel**. It has a long and a short sound.

Its **long** sound is the same as its name. Its **short** sound makes the sound heard inside 'pig.'

A. Record the name of each picture on the line. **Circle** the words that have the **short** 'i' sound.

B. Say the name of each picture. **Colour** the pictures with the short vowel 'i' sound.

Name: _____   Day 3 | Week 4

The letter 'u' is a vowel. It has a long and short sound.

Its long sound is the same as its name. Its short sound makes the sound heard inside 'duck.'

A. **Record** the name of each picture on the line. **Circle** the words that have the **short 'u'** sound.

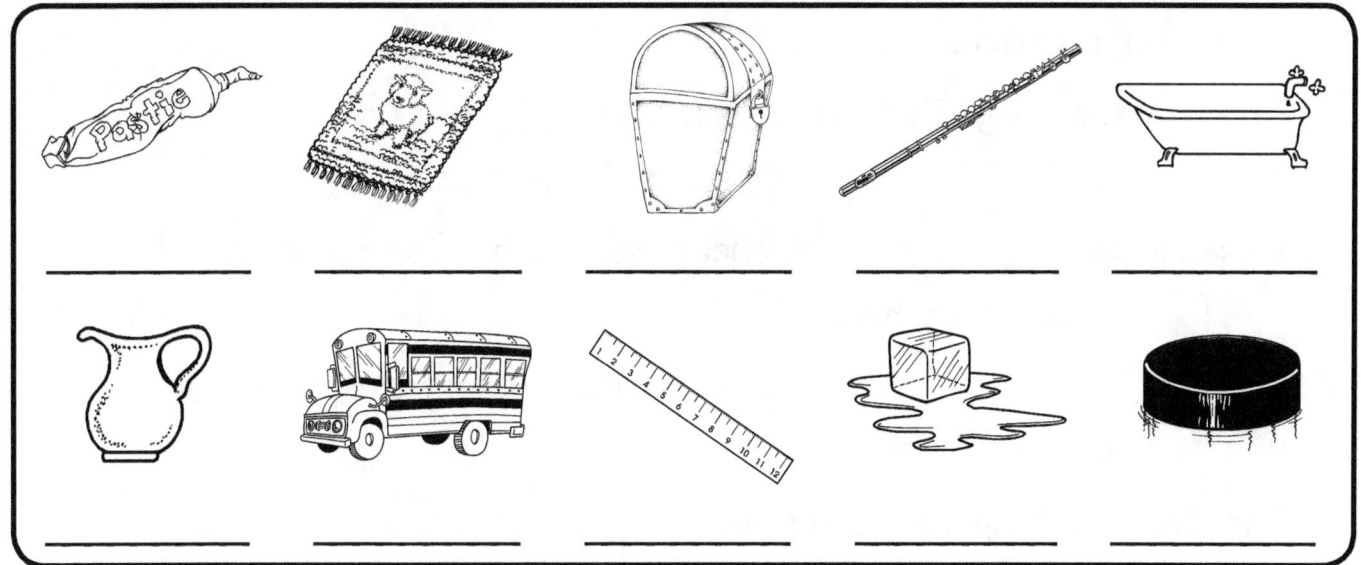

B. **Say** the name of each picture. **Colour** the pictures with the short vowel **'u.'**

Name: _____ Day 4 | Week 4

The vowels 'a, u, and i' each make **two** sounds.

One is a **long** sound and one is a **short** sound.

Complete each sentence with the correct word.

1. It is _____ to play on the swings at a park.
   (fin, fan, fun)

2. Put all of the things that you bought in this _____.
   (big, bug, bag)

3. I like to eat _____ and cheese sandwiches for my lunch.
   (him, ham, hum)

4. Did you _____ all the doors before you went to school.
   (lick, lock, luck)

5. The ship hit a large rock and slowly _____ to the ocean bottom.
   (sink, sank, sunk)

6. The little red hen liked to _____ at the seeds on the ground.
   (pick, pack, peck)

7. The angry police dog _____ the man in his leg to make him stop.
   (bit, bat, but)

8. The _____ suddenly flew past the goalie into the back of the net.
   (pick, puck, pack)

9. The magician's _____ surprised everyone watching the show.
   (trick, track, truck)

10. The _____ above the water made it hard to see where to travel with your boat. (mast, must, mist)

Name: _____   Day 5 | Week 4

A. Auditory Test on the Short Vowels 'a, u, and i'

1. a i u	2. a i u	3. a i u	4. a i u	5. a i u
6. a i u	7. a i u	8. a i u	9. a i u	10. a i u

B. Visual Discrimination Test on the Short Vowels 'a, u, and i'

picnic	quack	bridge	jingle	pump
suds	match	buds	fist	trunk

1. The three billy goats tried to walk across the troll's _____.

2. Jeff punched Nick in the face with his _____.

3. In the spring _____ on trees turn into leaves.

4. The duck began to _____ loudly when it saw a fox sneaking about.

5. I went to the well to _____ water into a pail for the horses.

6. The bells on the sleigh began to _____ when the horses began to pull it.

7. I used a _____ to light the candles on my sister's birthday cake.

8. The sink was full of water with _____ floating on the top.

9. The old _____ was full of things made out of gold.

10. In the summer my family likes to _____ at a sandy beach.

Week 5: Recognition of Short Vowels 'o' and 'e'

Objective: To develop a strong recognition of the sounds made by the short vowels 'o' and 'e' and their usage in developing strong word attack skills.

Day 1: Record the following sentences on a chart: 1. The dog trotted across the dock to sniff at the frog. 2. The frog hopped on a log in the pond and waited for bugs to gobble. Have the students read both sentences. Which vowel sound do you hear and see many times in the words of the sentences. (short o) Have the students underline the words in each sentence. Discuss the long and short sound made by the letter 'o.' Play this listening exercise: Does the word that I say have the long 'o' or the short 'o'? **Words:** 1. block 2. store 3. pole 4. song 5. foggy 6. wrong 7. crow 8. toast 9. shock 10. soft 11. ghost 12. clock

Picture Key: Row 1: rock, pot, fox, sock Row 2: doll, dog, mop, frog Row 3: box, clock, top, log Row 4: block, lock, rods, pop

Activity Worksheet: Page 33 The students will record the name of each picture on the line. Answer Key: See Picture Key

Day 2: Review the short vowels 'a, i, u, and o' with this exercise. Which vowel sound do you hear in each word that I say. **Words:** milk, stamp, foggy, grin, thumb, stick, skull, flop

Activity Worksheet: Page 34 The students will complete each sentence with a word from the Word Box. **Answer Key:** 1. top 2. ham 3. dog 4. cot 5. cub 6. cab 7. dug 8. tap 9. cut 10. hum 11. limp 12. lump

Day 3: Record the following story on a chart. **Story:** Heather Hen lived in a henhouse at the edge of a farm. In her nest, she lay seven eggs. For several days Heather sat on the eggs to help them hatch. One evening she felt something pecking at her feathers. She stood up, looked into her nest and saw seven yellow chicks pecking at their shells trying to get out. Have the students read the story silently and aloud. Discuss the vowel sound heard in Heather Hen. What vowel sound do you see and hear inside the words? (short e) Draw to their attention that other words in the story have the same sound. Have the students say and underline the words in the story with the short e sound.

Activity Worksheet: Page 35 The students are to complete each sentence with a short vowel 'e' word found in the Word Box. **Answer Key:** 1. fed 2. wet 3. leg 4. beg 5. tell 6. ten 7. bed 8. well, test 9. men, went 10. eggs, nest 11. tent, when 12. bench

Day 4: Review the short vowels 'a, i, e, o, and u' with the following riddles. The students are to give the answer and to name the short vowel heard inside it. **Riddles:** 1. I am a machine that takes people up and down in large buildings. (elevator, short e) 2. I am a group of people who are friends and do things together. (gang, short a) 3. I am a kind of weather. You cannot see where you are going in me. (fog, short o) 4. I go over water. You have to use me to get to the other side. (bridge, short i) 5. I am part of a ladder. You step on me to go up and down. (rung, short u) 6. I am part of your face. I am found under your mouth. (chin, short i) 7. I am a sound that comes out of your mouth. It sounds like music. (whistle, short i) 8. I am made of wood. People park their boats beside me. (dock, short o) 9. I am a place to store things. I am also a part of an elephant. (trunk, short u) 10. Some men grow them on their chins. Santa has white ones. (whiskers, short i)

Picture Key: Row 1: jet, hand, mop, ship Row 2: nut, rock, swim, grin, Row 3: sock, bench, map, truck

Activity Worksheet: Page 36 The students are to record the name of each picture on the line under it. Some of the words will be used to complete the sentences. **Answer Key: A -** Row 1: jet, hand, mop, ship Row 2: nut, rock, swim, grin Row 3: sock, bench, map, truck **B -** 1. map 2. ship 3. jet 4. truck 5. rock 6. sock 7. grin 8. swim

Day 5: Auditory and Visual Discrimination Test on the Short Vowels 'a, e, i, o, u': Page 37

A. Auditory Test: The students are to record the short vowel heard in each word spoken by the teacher on the line in each box. **Words:** 1. drop 2. crib 3. crush 4. song 5. elf 6. smash 7. steps 8. crack 9. flop 10. bush
Answer Key: 1. o 2. i 3. u 4. o 5. e 6. a 7. e 8. a 9. o 10. u

B. Visual Discrimination Test: The student will complete each sentence with the correct word.
Answer Key: 1. tan 2. sang, song 3. flap 4. wall 5. bell 6. clip, clop 7. big, bug, bag 8. set, sit 9. will, well 10. dog, dig

Name: _____ Day 1 | Week 5

The letter 'o' is a **vowel**. It has a **long** and a **short** sound.

Its **long sound** is the same as its name and its **short sound** makes the sound heard in 'dog' and 'frog.'

Record the name of each picture on the line.

_____ _____ _____ _____

_____ _____ _____ _____

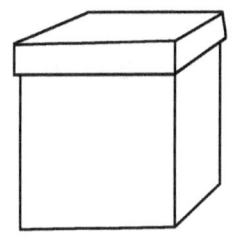   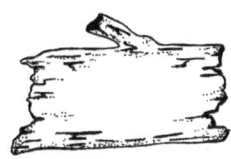

_____ _____ _____ _____

  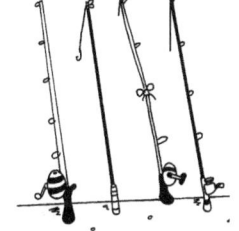 

_____ _____ _____ _____

Name: _____   Day 2 | Week 5

The short vowels '**a**, **i**, **u**, and **o**' are heard in many words.

Examples: cap, tin, bump, dog

A. Make **two** new words by changing the vowel sound in the following words.

Word Box

1. cat _____ _____   4. cob _____ _____

2. lamp _____ _____   5. tip _____ _____

3. dig _____ _____   6. him _____ _____

B. Use the words that you made to complete the following sentences.

1. I like to watch my _____ spin around and around on the floor.

2. Today I have a _____ and cheese sandwich in my lunch box.

3. The little _____ barked loudly at the people walking by his yard.

4. I slept on a _____ in a tent at summer camp.

5. The little _____ followed the mother bear everywhere she went.

6. Dad paid the driver for his ride in the _____.

7. My mother _____ holes in her garden and planted her flowers.

8. There is no water coming out of the _____.

9. I used a sharp knife to _____ out a face in the pumpkin.

10. The little boy liked to _____ many tunes.

11. The old man hurt his leg and had to _____ all the way home.

12. When John fell he got a big _____ on the back of his head.

Name: _____   Day 3 | Week 5

The **short vowel 'e'** has the sound heard in the words sh**e**ll, w**e**nt, dr**e**ss and p**e**t

Complete each sentence with a word from the Word Box.

Word Box							
bench	eggs	nest	well	ten	beg	when	wet
test	tell	leg	fed	men	tent	went	bed

1. The mother bird _____ her babies fat juicy worms for food.

2. Today it is _____ and cloudy outside.

3. How did you hurt your _____ ?

4. My dog likes to sit and _____ for his treats.

5. _____ us all about your shopping trip in the city of Toronto.

6. Tony used _____ sheets of paper to make his storybook.

7. Don't forget to make your _____ before you go to school.

8. You did very _____ on your spelling _____.

9. The two _____ _____ to the rink to watch the hockey game.

10. The big brown hen laid two _____ in her _____.

11. We will sleep in a _____ _____ we go camping.

12. I sat on a _____ at the park and watched the swans on the pond.

Name: _____   Day 4 | Week 5

Remember the sound made by the short vowels 'a, e, i, o, u.'

Examples: camp, tent, cot, fire, bugs

A. Under each picture, record its name.

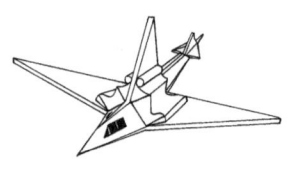	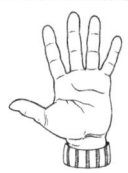		
_____	_____	_____	_____

_____	_____	_____	_____

_____	_____	_____	_____

B. Complete each sentence with a picture word.

1. We used a _____ to find the city of Ottawa.

2. The huge _____ slowly moved beside the dock.

3. The big _____ landed on the runway safely.

4. The large red _____ was loaded with many boxes.

5. The huge black _____ rolled all the way down the high hill.

6. Did you lose your blue _____ under your bed yesterday?

7. The happy little boy had a big _____ on his face.

8. I like to _____ in our swimming pool on hot days in the summer.

Name: _____   Day 5 | Week 5

A. Auditory Test on the Short Vowels 'a, e, i, o, u'

1. _____	2. _____	3. _____	4. _____	5. _____
6. _____	7. _____	8. _____	9. _____	10. _____

B. Visual Discrimination Test on the Short Vowels 'a, e, i, o, u'

1. Some people like to lie in the sun to get a _____.
   (tin, ten, tan)

2. We _____ a _____ about three little kittens.
   (sing, sang, sung, song)

3. Birds must _____ their wings quickly when they fly.
   (flop, flap, flip)

4. The _____ around the castle was made of red bricks.
   (will, wall, well)

5. Did you hear the church _____ ring this morning.
   (bill, ball, bell)

6. The horse's hooves went _____ _____ on the road.
   (clip, clap, clop)

7. I caught a _____ _____ in a paper _____.
   (big, bag, bug, beg)

8. Will you please _____ the table for supper and _____ down.
   (sit, set, sat)

9. I _____ get some water from the _____.
   (well, will, wall)

10. My _____ likes to _____ holes in our backyard.
    (dug, dig, dog)

Week 6: Reviewing Long and Short Vowels

Objective: To strengthen and review the recognition of the long and short vowels 'a, e, i, o, u'

Day 1: On a chart record the following sentences. <u>Sentences:</u> 1. <u>Please</u> gather all the <u>leaves</u> with the <u>green</u> rake. 2. <u>Tony</u> read a book about <u>boats</u>, <u>deep seas</u>, and lands that were far away. 3. Lisa put the <u>five roses</u> in a vase and <u>placed</u> it on the <u>table</u>. 4. In the autumn, the wind <u>makes</u> the <u>leaves</u> dance on the <u>blades</u> of grass. 5. The puppy dug a <u>deep hole</u> in the dirt to <u>hide</u> his <u>bone</u>. Have the students underline each word in the sentences that have the long vowel sound. Review the two rules about long vowels. **Rule 1:** When a word ends with an 'e' the vowel inside the word is usually long. **Rule 2:** When two vowels are seen together in a word, the first vowel is long and the second one is silent. Have the students locate the words that each rule is talking about and underline them.

Activity Worksheet: Page 39 **A.** The students will match the vowel rule to the word. **Answer Key: A.** 1. Rule 2 2. Rule 1 3. Rule 2 4. Rule 1 5. Rule 2 6. Rule 2 7. Rule 2 8. Rule 2 9. Rule 1 10. Rule 1 11. Rule 2 12. Rule 1 **B.** 1. o 2. e 3. o 4. i 5. i 6. o 7. u 8. e 9. a 10. o 11. a 12. a 13. a 14. a 15. e

Day 2: Review the sounds made by the long and short vowels using these clues. 1. I have two wheels, two pedals and one seat. I am a (bike). 2. It begins as a bud on a tree every spring. It is a (leaf). 3. A top can do this on the floor. (spin) 4. A dog likes to dig one in the ground. (hole) 5. Toothpaste is found inside one. (tube) 6. Children like to chew it and blow bubbles. (gum) 7. It is a coat without sleeves. (cape) 8. It is put on a letter. (stamp) 9. It is the opposite to hard. (soft) 10. It is a place to sleep outside. (tent)

Picture Key: Row 1: snake, tree, cone, vine, tube Row 2: tub, steps, rock, crab, hair Row 3: rain, bike, net, leaf, bone

Activity Worksheet: Page 40 **A.** The students are to spell the name of each picture. **B.** Change the words to long vowel words. **Answer Key: A.** Row 1: snake, tree, cone, vine, tube Row 2: tub, stairs, rock, crab, hair Row 3: rain, bike, net, leaf, bone **B.** 1. cape 2. tube 3. goat 4. hide 5. rain 6. cube 7. hope 8. read 9. tape 10. huge 11. feed 12. kite

Day 3: Review the long and short vowels with these rddles. The students are to name the answer and the vowel sound heard in each one. **Riddles:** 1. I am round, fat, and pink in colour. I live in a pen. What am I? (pig, short i) 2. I am part of an animal. I may be long, furry, short or curly. What am I? (tail, long a) 3. You can build things with them. Each one is shaped like a cube. What are they called? (blocks, short o) 4. I am a small musical instrument. A man called the Pied Piper led people away with its music. What is it called? (flute, long u) 5. It is an ocean animal that lives in a shell. What is it called? (clam, short a) 6. It is a place to sit and eat during the summer outside of your house. What is it called? (deck, short e) 7. It is a plant that loves to climb on fences and walls. What is it called? (vine, long i) 8. It is a dark yellow. It is found in the middle of an egg. What is it called? (yolk, long o) 9. It is a little wind. It may make you feel warm or cool. What is it called? (breeze, long e) 10. It is a round fruit that grows on a tree. It may be green or purple. What is it called? (plum, short u)

Activity Worksheet: Page 41 The students are to circle each short vowel word in each column.
Answer Key: Row a - sand, last, ask, wax, cab, lap, jam, gas **Row i:** hill, lift, big, miss, fix, lick, pick **Row e:** men, elf, pen, pelt, tent, web, neck, desk **Row o:** toss, box, job, block, rock, dog, lost, pop, hot **Row u:** bug, rust, hum, cub, nuts, bun, tub

Day 4: Review long and short vowels heard in compound words. On a chart record the following compound words in a column. Beside each compound word print the two words that make it and discuss the vowel sounds heard in each one. **Compound Words:** airline, bareback, bulldog, cupcake, fireplace, flashlight, goldfish, haystack, pancake, pigtails

Activity Worksheet: Page 42 The students are to record the vowel sound heard in each part of the compound word. **Answer Key:** 1. long a; long a 2. long a; long e 3. short u; long o 4. long o; short i 5. long i; long a 6. short e; short a 7. short u; long a 8. short a; short o 9. short u; short e 10. short a; long a 11. long e; short u 12. short i; short i

Day 5: Auditory and Visual Discrimination Test on Long and Short Vowel Sounds: Page 43

A. Auditory Test: The teacher will say the word for each box and the students will listen and fill in the missing vowel sounds. **Words:** 1. apron 2. button 3. icicle 4. giant 5. behind 6. bench 7. elastic 8. umbrella 9. music 10. rope 11. unicorn 12. picnic **Answer Key:** 1. a,o 2. u, o 3. i, i 4. i, a 5. e, i 6. e 7. e, a, i 8. u, e. o 9. u, i 10. o 11. u, i, o 12. i, i

Visual Discrimination Test: The students will classify the words in the box under the vowel sound heard in each one. **Answer Key:** *Long a:* mail, wave *Long e:* peep, beam, leap *Long i:* time, glide, pipe *Long o:* nose, load, cone *Long u:* tube, cute, mule *Short a:* tramp, wax, rash *Short e:* shell, felt, smell *Short i:* lick, pinch, thick *Short o:* pop, soft, lock *Short u:* hut, plump, luck

Name: _____   Day 1 | Week 6

Syllables are parts of words.

Remember these rules:

1. If a one syllable word has two vowels, the first vowel often has the long sound and the second vowel is silent. **Examples:** boat, seal

2. If a word ends with an '**e**', the vowel before it is usually a long vowel. **Examples:** fine, save

A. Which rule does each word follow? Is it **Rule 1** or **Rule 2**?

1. pure _____
2. fear _____
3. June _____
4. deep _____
5. wife _____
6. note _____

7. vase _____
8. mule _____
9. heel _____
10. goat _____
11. fire _____
12. least _____

B. Complete each word with its missing vowel.

1. b ___ ne
2. d ___ ep
3. g ___ at
4. h ___ de
5. f ___ ne

6. j ___ ke
7. f ___ el
8. k ___ ep
9. c ___ ke
10. b ___ ne

11. r ___ ke
12. p ___ il
13. g ___ me
14. ch ___ ir
15. sh ___ ep

Name: _____   Day 2 | Week 6

Did you know that you can change **short** vowel words into words with **long** vowels?

Here's how!

You can add an '**e**' to the end of the word that makes the vowel ahead shout out its own long sound or you can add a **vowel** to make a long vowel **pair**.

Examples: can - cane; hat - hate; rod - road; bet - beet

A. Record the word on the line that matches each picture.

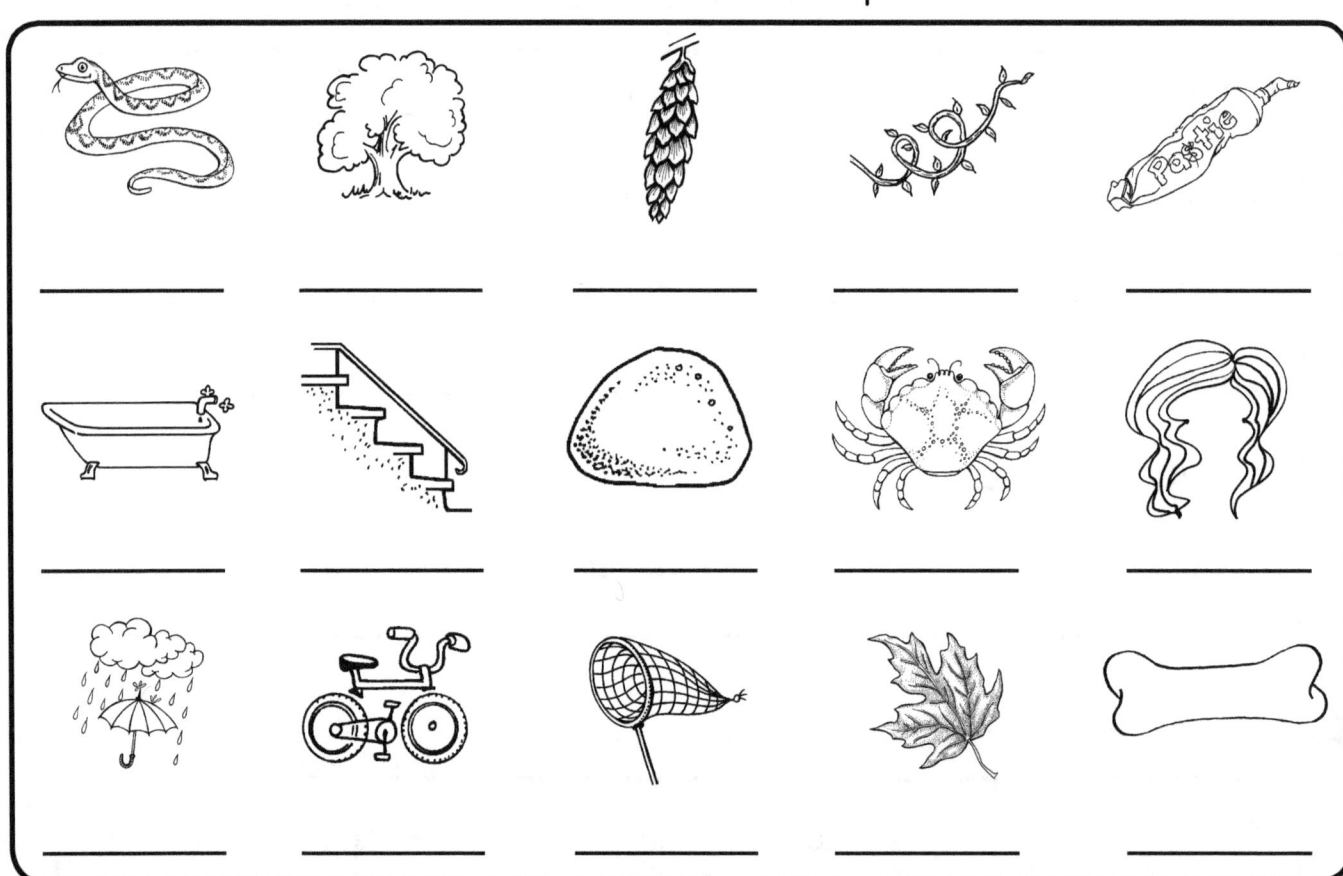

B. Make each word a **long** vowel word.

1. cap _____
2. tub _____
3. got _____
4. hid _____

5. ran _____
6. cub _____
7. hop _____
8. red _____

7. tap _____
10. hug _____
11. fed _____
12. kit _____

Name: _____ Day 3 | Week 6

Long and short vowels make different sounds.

Remember:

Long vowels say their own names.

Short vowels make different sounds.

Examples: Long Vowels - game, comb, tube, ice, eel

Short Vowels - tub, big, bend, fox, ran

Circle each word that has the **short vowel** sound in each column.

a	i	e	o	u
pain	hike	leap	toss	pure
sand	hill	men	box	bug
last	lift	elf	job	rust
ate	dime	pen	road	use
ask	big	deep	block	hum
tail	hide	pelt	goat	tube
name	miss	peel	rock	cub
wax	pine	tent	dog	nuts
cab	pipe	seem	note	cube
lap	fix	web	pop	cute
tame	lick	feel	lost	bun
jam	time	neck	bone	tune
gas	pick	peak	hot	tub
mail	ride	desk	home	rule

Name: _____ | Day 4 | Week 6

A **compound** word is made of **two** words.

Examples: scarecrow, buttercup, railroad, highway

Compound words often have **two** vowel sounds that you can hear.

Example: scare - long a sound; crow - long o sound

On the lines beside each compound word record the vowel sound heard in each part.

Compound words have two vowel sounds.

Example: driveway   long i   long a

1. airplane
2. daydream
3. tugboat
4. goldfish
5. fireplace
6. breakfast
7. cupcake
8. grasshopper
9. sunset
10. pancake
11. peanut
12. windmill

Name: _____   Day 5 | Week 6

A. Auditory Test on the Long and Short Vowel Sounds 'a, e, i, o, u'

1. ___ pr ___ n	2. b ___ tt ___ n	3. ___ c ___ cle
4. g ___ ___ nt	5. b ___ h ___ nd	6. b ___ nch
7. ___ l ___ t ___ c	8. ___ mbr ___ ll ___	9. m ___ s ___ c
10. r ___ pe	11. ___ n ___ c ___ rn	12. p ___ c n ___ c

B. Visual Discrimination Test on the Long and Short Vowels 'a, e, i, o, u'

```
mail    peep    rash    tramp   leap    tag
lick    soft    hut     felt    load    cone
tube    wax     plump   thick   shell   cute
pinch   wave    nose    pipe    beam    pop
lock    luck    glide   time    smell   mule
```

Long a	Long e	Long i	Long o	Long u
_____	_____	_____	_____	_____
_____	_____	_____	_____	_____
_____	_____	_____	_____	_____
Short a	Short e	Short i	Short o	Short u
_____	_____	_____	_____	_____
_____	_____	_____	_____	_____
_____	_____	_____	_____	_____

Week 7: Recognition of 'Yy' as a Vowel and as a Consonant

Objective: To reinforce the recognition of 'y' as a vowel and a consonant and to strengthen their usage.

Day 1: Record the following words on a chart: you, yes, yell, your. Have the students say all the words. Discuss the initial sound, its position in a word, and its name. Record these words on the chart: fry, try, dry, sky. Have the students say the words. Discuss the sound made at the end of each word. What sound does the letter 'y' say at the end of each word. (long i) When the letter 'y' makes the same sound as a vowel at the end of a word, it becomes a vowel. When the 'y' is a vowel it makes the long 'i' vowel sound.

Picture Key: Row 1: yarn, sky, cry, yoyo Row 2: yolk, fly, yawn, frying pan

Activity Worksheet: Page 45 **A.** The students will record the correct name for the sound heard by the letter 'y' in each word. **Answer Key: A -** Row 1: consonant, vowel, vowel, consonant Row 2: consonant, vowel, consonant, vowel **B -** The students are to record the word in the box to match each clue. **Answer Key:** 1. sly 2. young 3. reply 4. yank 5. rhyme 6. cyclone 7. yawn 8. fry

Day 2: Record the following words on a chart: cry, sky, buy, fly. The students are to read the words and to listen to their final sounds. What sound is heard at the end of each word? (long i) What letter is making the long 'i' sound? (y) Remind your students that when 'y' is found at the end of a one syllable word, it becomes a vowel and makes the long 'i' sound. On the chart record the following words: baby, funny, happy, shiny. Have the students read the words and to listen to their final sounds. What sound is the letter 'y' making at the end of each word. (long e) Explain that when 'y' appears at the end of a two syllable word, the 'y' makes the long 'e' vowel sound.

Activity Worksheet: Page 46 **A.** The students will classify each word to the vowel sound made by the letter 'y.' **B.** The students will use the words in Part A to complete the sentences. **Answer Key:** <u>Part A</u> - 1. long i 2. long e 3. long i 4. long e 5. long i 6. long e 7. long e 8. long e 9. long i 10. long e 11. long e 12. long e 13. long i 14. long e 15. long e <u>Part B:</u> 1. fly, every 2. fluffy, bunny, swiftly 3. hurry, grocery 4. try, rhyme 5. story, family

Day 3: Review '**Yy**' as a vowel and as a consonant using this activity. Listen to each word that I say. In each word there is the letter 'Yy.' Is it being used as a vowel or as a consonant? 1. many (V) 2. yawn (C) 3. spy (V) 4. yard (C) 5. pretty (V) 6. ready (V) 7. year (C) 8. dry (V) 9. pretty (V) 10. yank (C) What vowel sound do you hear in: many - long e; spy - long i; pretty - long e; ready - long e; dry - long i; pretty - long e

Picture Key: Row 1: fairy, yard, puppy, yawn, yo-yo Row 2: sky, spy, yarn, sunny, bunny

Activity Worksheet: Page 47 **A.** The students will record the word for each picture on the line. **B.** The students will classify the sounds that 'Y' makes in words. **Answer Key: A.** Row 1: fairy, yard, puppy, yawn, yo-yo Row 2: sky, spy, yarn, sunny, bunny B. 1. LI 2. C 3. LI 4. LI 5. LE 6. LE 7. LE 8. LE 9. C 10. LI 11. C 12. LE 13. C 14. LE 15. LE

Day 4: Review the sounds made by the letter '**y**' with these words. Say each word clearly and have the students locate the name of the sound heard in each one. Record on a chart the following headings: Y as the Vowel 'i'; Y as the vowel 'e'; Y as a consonant. Words: 1. history 2. yank 3. cycle 4. spicy 5. yacht 6. style 7. yodel 8. study 9. yawn 10. reply

Activity Worksheet: Page 48 The students will read the story called 'Canada's Favourite Sport' and then reread it to locate words with 'Y' as the vowel 'i' ; 'Y' as the vowel 'e' and 'Y' as a consonant. **Answer Key:** 'Y' as the Vowel 'i': by, sky, dry, style, fly; 'Y' as the Vowel 'e' : hockey, very, busy, early, steady, icy, sturdy, shiny, carry, quickly, ready; 'Y' as a Consonant: young, backyard, player, player's, played, boys

Day 5: Auditory Test on the Short 'Y' , Long 'Y' and the Consonant 'Y': Page 49 The students are to circle the sound that the letter 'Y' makes in each word spoken by the teacher. **Words:** 1. yawn 2. cycle 3. jerky 4. pry 5. canary 6. young 7. valley 8. rhyme **Answer Key:** 1. Consonant Y 2. Long i 3. Long e 4. Long i 5. Long e 6. Consonant Y 7. Long e 8. Long i

B. Visual Discrimination Test on Y as a Vowel and as a Consonant: The students are to box the words that have the consonant Y; underline the words that have 'Y' as the long vowel 'e'; circle the words that have 'y' as the long vowel 'i'. **Answer Key:** 1. underline 2. circle 3. box 4. underline 5. underline 6. box 7. circle 8. underline 9. circle 10. underline 11. box 12. underline 13. circle 14. underline 15. underline 16. circle 17. underline 18. circle 19. underline 20. box 21. underline 22. circle 23. circle 24. box

Name: _____ Day 1 | Week 7

Don't forget these rules!

The letter 'Yy' is called a **consonant** at the **beginning** of a word.

Example: yard

The letter 'Yy' is called a **vowel** when it makes the **long 'i'** sound at the **end** of a word.

Example: fly

A. Is the letter 'Yy' a consonant or the long vowel 'i' in each word. Record the word 'consonant' or 'vowel' on the line under each picture.

B. Record the word in the box on the line to match each meaning.

fry   cyclone   yank   young   sly   reply   rhyme   yawn

1. sneaky, tricky _____
2. the opposite to old _____
3. to answer someone _____
4. to pull something quickly _____
5. words that sound the same at the end _____
6. a very windy storm _____
7. a sign that you are feeling tired _____
8. a way to cook meat _____

Name: _____   Day 2 | Week 7

Remember these rules:

1. When 'Yy' comes at the **end** of a word, it becomes a **vowel**.
2. When 'Yy' is the **only** vowel at the end of a **one syllable** word it makes the **long 'i'** sound. **Examples:** by, try, cry
3. When 'Yy' is the only vowel at the end of a word that has **more than one syllable**, it makes the **long 'e'** sound. **Examples:** hurry, story, bunny

A. Read each word below carefully. Beside each one record 'L I' if 'Y' makes the **long 'i'** sound and 'L E' if 'Y' makes the **long 'e'** sound.

1. cry _____
2. bunny _____
3. why _____
4. swiftly _____
5. fly _____

6. family _____
7. grocery _____
8. history _____
9. try _____
10. silently _____

11. every _____
12. hurry _____
13. rhyme _____
14. story _____
15. fluffy _____

B. Use the words in the above lists to complete the sentences.

1. A _____ is an insect that buzzes around food _____ day in the summer.

2. The _____ _____ hopped _____ towards the woods.

3. We had to _____ to get to the _____ store before it closed.

4. I _____ to write poems that _____.

5. The _____ about the poor _____ made me feel sad.

Name: _____   Day 3 | Week 7

Remember:

Sometimes the letter 'Yy' is a **consonant**. **Example:** yellow

Sometimes it is a **vowel**. **Example:** my - long i or bunny - long e

A. Match each word to its picture.

| bunny | yoyo | sunny | yawn | spy |
| yard | sky | yarn | fairy | puppy |

B. On the line, beside each word, record **C** if 'Yy' is used as a **consonant**; **LI** if 'Yy' has the **long 'i'** sound; **LE** if 'Yy' has the **long 'e'** sound.

1. cry   ____
2. you   ____
3. sly   ____
4. dry   ____
5. candy ____

6. every ____
7. windy ____
8. lovely ____
9. your   ____
10. try   ____

11. yes   ____
12. pretty ____
13. yell   ____
14. happy ____
15. many   ____

Name: _____   Day 4 | Week 7

Read the story about Canada's favourite sport.

Look for and record words with the **consonant 'y'**, the **vowel 'y'** that makes the **long 'e' sound** and the **vowel 'y'** that makes the **long 'i'** sound.

Underline the words in the story and record them in the correct column.

Canada's Favourite Sport

In Canada, hockey is a very busy sport. The game is played by young boys and girls and men and women. Children learn to skate at an early age. This makes them strong and steady skaters. Hockey is played on icy ponds under a blue sky, on backyard rinks and in clean, dry arenas.

Each player, on a team, wears the same style of sweater, stockings and pants called a uniform. A shiny helmet is worn on the player's head and strong, sturdy skates are worn on the player's feet. Each player has to carry a hockey stick. It is used to quickly shoot a shiny black puck into the net past the ready and waiting goalie. If the puck is able to fly past the goalie, a goal will be scored.

Y as the Vowel i	Y as the Vowel e	Y as a Consonant

Name: _____   Day 5 | Week 7

A. Auditory Test on 'Y' as a 'Vowel' and as a 'Consonant'

1. Long i Long e Consonant Y	2. Long i Long e Consonant Y	3. Long i Long e Consonant Y	4. Long i Long e Consonant Y
5. Long i Long e Consonant Y	6. Long i Long e Consonant Y	7. Long i Long e Consonant Y	8. Long i Long e Consonant Y

B. Visual Discrimination Test on 'Y' as a Vowel and as a Consonant

yak   party   fry

1. icy
2. sly
3. yell
4. lucky
5. frisky
6. year
7. cycle
8. carry

9. July
10. dirty
11. yank
12. country
13. good-bye
14. thirsty
15. funny
16. sky

17. snowy
18. myself
19. frisky
20. yet
21. tiny
22. reply
23. try
24. yawn

Week 8: Recognition of 'ar, er, ir, or, ur' in words

Objective: To make students aware that the letter '**r**' often works with vowels to make one sound in words.

Day 1: On a chart record the following words: car, corn, river, burn, girl. Discuss how the words have similar sounds. What sound do you hear in each word? (r) What sound is directly in front of each 'r'? (a vowel) Record the sounds 'ar, or, ir, ur, and er' on the chart. Discuss the sounds that they make. In the sounds '**ur**, **ir**, and **er**', only the consonant '**r**' is heard; **ar** says the name of the **consonant 'r'**; '**or**' says the word '**or**.'

Picture Key: Row 1: horn, bird, tiger, church Row 2: star, cork, circle, turkey

Activity Worksheet: Page 51 **A.** The students are to complete each word under the picture with a vowel and the letter 'r.' **B.** Each word is to be completed with the correct vowel + 'r' blend. **Answer Key: A.** Row 1: or, ir, er, ur Row 2: ar, or, ir, ur **B.** 1. ir, or, ir, ar 2. er, or, ar, ur 3. or, ir, er, er 4. ur, ar, or, ar 5. er, ur, ur, ar 6. er, ur, ar, ir 7. ir, er, or, or

Day 2; Review the **vowel + 'r'** blends with your students. On a chart record the sounds '**ar, er, ir, or, ur**' across the top. Under these sounds record the following groups of words:
1. f__m, f__m, f__m (ar, or, ir) 2. b__n, b__n, b__n (or, ar, ur) 3. sh__t, sh__t (or, ir) 4. f__, f__, f__, f__ (ir, or, ur, ar) 5. st__, st__ (ar, ir) 6. t__e, t__e (or, ir) 7. c__d, c__d (ar, or) Have the students complete each group of words and say them.

Activity Worksheet: Page 52 The students are to record the correct word to complete each sentence. **Answer Key:** 1. organ, church 2. whirls, yards 3. forgot, stir 4. purple, flower 5. hurt, horse 6. mother, bird 7. shirt, birthday 8. farmer, corn 9. turtle, river 10. afternoon, teacher, story 11. fur, thicker 12. corner, store

Day 3: Review the '**vowel + r blends**' using these clues. Have the students record the answers on a chart and to circle the 'vowel + r blend.' **Clues:** 1. It joins your hand to your body. (arm) 2. Playing in mud can make you look this way. (dirty) 3. It is a loud sound heard in a storm. (thunder) 4. It is the opposite to long. (short) 5. A fire does this to wood. (burn) 6. You may get one in the mail. (letter)

Activity Worksheet: Page 53 **A.** The students will circle the '**vowel + r blend**' and then use it to make a new word. **B.** The students will complete each sentence with words from the list. **Answer Key: A.** 1. ir; first 2. er; better 3. ir; dirt 4. ar; part 5. or; cork 6. or; for 7. ur; turtle 8. ar; harm; 9. er; butter 10. ir; dirt 11. ur; curl 12. ir; fir **B.** 1. start 2. derby 3. birthday 4. market 5. nurse 6. storm 7. cord 8. sparkle

Day 4: On a chart record the **vowel + 'r'** blends across the top. Below the sounds record the following incomplete words: 1. f ir st 2. butt er 3. n ur se 4. d ar k 5. c or k 6. d ir t 7. p or k 8. st or m 9. fing er 10. t or n Have the students record a vowel + 'r' blend to complete each word.

Activity Worksheet: Page 54 **A.** Students are to circle all the vowel + 'r' blends in each sentence. **B.** The circled words are to be classified under the vowel + 'r' blend that each one contains. **Answer Key: A.** 1. bird, wire, thirsty 2. purse, church, River 3. pitchfork, horses, dinner 4. spark, carpet, fire 5. circus, marching 6. warm, surf, afternoon 7. orchard, large 8. turkey, bird, feathers **B. ar Words:** spark, carpet, marching, warm, large; **er Words:** river, dinner, afternoon, feathers; **ir Words:** bird, wire, thirsty, fire, circus; **or Words:** pitchfork, horses, orchard; **ur Words:** purse, church, surf, turkey

Day 5: Auditory Test on the 'Vowel + r Blends': Page 55 The students are to record the Vowel + 'r' blend heard in each word said by the teacher on the line in each box. **Words:** 1. sharp 2. more 3. twirl 4. burst 5. core 6. party 7. skirt 8. burst 9. sore 10. sliver **Answer Key:** 1. ar 2. or 3. ir 4. ur 5. or 6. ar 7. ir 8. ur 9. or 10. er

Visual Discrimination Test: The students are to complete each sentence with the correct word. **Answer Key:** 1. fork 2. lower 3. scar 4. circle 5. curls 6. chores 7. tower 8. army 9. twirl 10. churn

Name: _____   Day 1 | Week 8

Sometimes a vowel and a consonant will become partners in a word and make a sound together.

Examples: ar - farm; er - river; ir - girl; or - fork; ur - burn

A. Complete each picture word with one of these sounds: ar, er, ir, or, ur

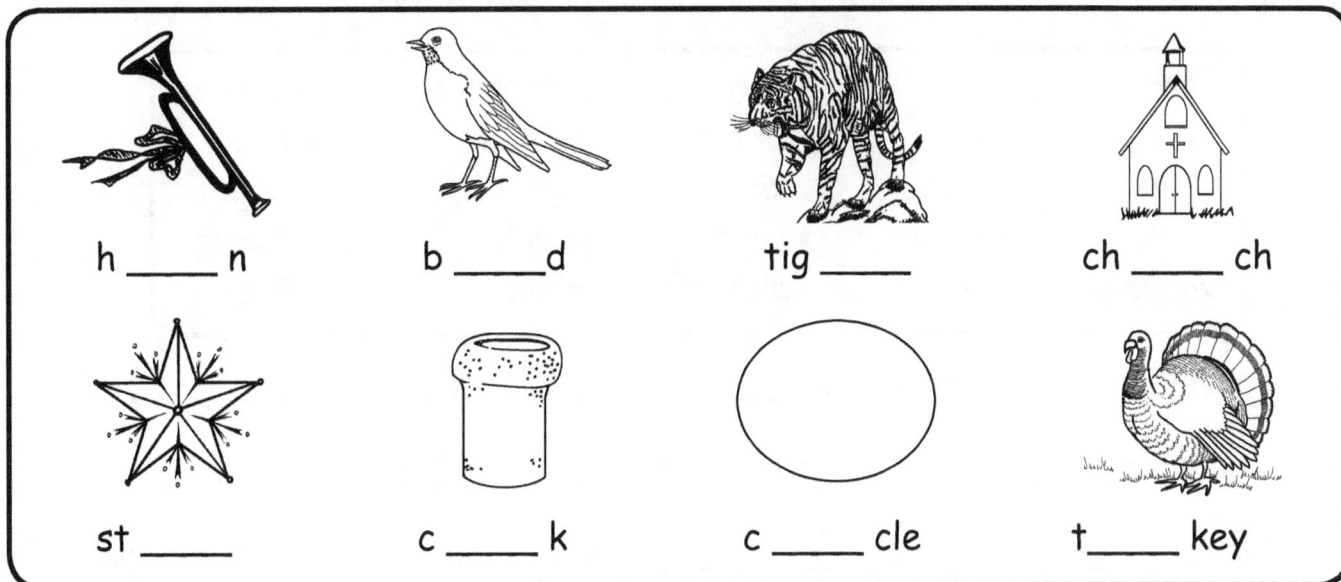

h ___ n   b ___ d   tig ___   ch ___ ch

st ___   c ___ k   c ___ cle   t ___ key

B. Complete each word by recording 'ar, er, ir, or, ur' on the line.

1.	g ___ l	c ___ k	sk ___ t	sc ___ f
2.	moth ___	h ___ n	j ___	t ___ key
3.	c ___ n	b ___ d	pap ___	slipp ___
4.	p ___ se	b ___ n	st ___ m	g ___ den
5.	ladd ___	t ___ tle	ch ___ ch	y ___ d
6.	lett ___	n ___ se	sp ___ kle	th ___ d
7.	c ___ cle	j ___ k	f ___ ty	n ___ th

Name: _____   Day 2 | Week 8

Don't forget the sounds that '**ar, er, ir, or** and **ur**' make in words. They may be found at the **beginning**, in the **middle**, and at the **end** of words.

Examples: order (B), horn (M), for (E)

Complete each sentence using a word from the Word Box.

corner	fur	store	afternoon	teacher
story	thicker	turtle	farmer	river
shirt	mother	corn	birthday	forgot
hurt	horse	bird	purple	flower
yards	stir	whirls	organ	church

1. Tammy is able to play the big _____ in her _____.

2. The wind _____ leaves all over _____ in the fall.

3. Nancy _____ to _____ the soup and it stuck to the pan.

4. That wild _____ _____ is called a violet.

5. Lisa did not get _____ when she fell off her _____.

6. A _____ _____ is never far away from her babies in their nest.

7. Mark got a red _____ for his _____.

8. The _____ ploughed his fields so he could plant some _____.

9. The little _____ hid under a rock near the _____.

10. In the _____ our _____ reads us a _____.

11. My cat's _____ gets _____ when winter comes.

12. On the _____ of our street there is a grocery _____.

Name: _____   Day 3 | Week 8

How well can you spell words using 'ar, er, ir, or, and ur'?

A. Circle the **ar, er, ir, or** and **ur** in each word and then write a new word using the same sound.

Example: st⊙ne, storm

1. fir	f ___ st	7. purple	t ___ tle
2. never	bett ___	8. barn	h ___ m
3. third	d ___ t	9. letter	butt ___
4. dark	p ___ t	10. third	d ___ t
5. born	c ___ k	11. burn	c ___ l
6. corn	f ___	12. girl	f ___

B. Complete each sentence using a word from the box.

> cord   birthday   market   nurse   start   storm   derby   sparkle

1. Tony will _____ on his trip to the city this morning.

2. Jeff and his horse tried to win first place in the _____.

3. I gave my mother a purse and a card for her _____.

4. My mother went to the _____ to buy some fruit and vegetables.

5. A _____ looked at the big bump on the girl's head.

6. The bus driver had to drive the children home during a big snow _____.

7. A strong _____ was used to close the box.

8. The lights on the tree _____ and glow at Christmas.

Name: _____   Day 4 | Week 8

How well do you look at the sounds in words?

A. **Read** each sentence carefully and circle all the words in each one that contain '**ar, er, ir, or,** and **ur**.'

1. The pet bird in the wire cage was thirsty.

2. A purse was found in front of a church on River Street.

3. Tom used his pitchfork to give the horses good hay for their dinner.

4. A spark from a match fell onto the carpet and caused a fire.

5. The circus people were led into the ring by a marching band.

6. We walked in the warm sandy surf at the beach one afternoon.

7. At an orchard we found some large, round apples.

8. A turkey is a big bird with black feathers and a red head.

B. Record the words from the sentences that contain a '**vowel + r blend**' on the lines in the boxes.

ar	er	ir	or	ur

Name: _____   Day 5 | Week 8

A. Auditory Test on the Vowel + r Blends

1. ____	2. ____	3. ____	4. ____	5. ____
6. ____	7. ____	8. ____	9. ____	10. ____

B. Visual Discrimination Test on Vowel + r Blends in Words

Words

| churn | twirl | army | tower | chores |
| fork | scar | lower | curls | circle |

1. We use a knife and a _____ to eat our food.

2. The stairs took us to a _____ floor.

3. The cut on the boy's cheek left a _____.

4. We stood in a _____ to play the game.

5. Some girls like to have _____ put in their hair.

6. On a farm children have many _____ to do each day.

7. A _____ is a very tall building that can be seen for long distances.

8. Soldiers in the _____ marched quickly behind the loud band.

9. The young girl could _____ her baton quickly to the music.

10. Years ago people used a _____ to make their butter.

Week 9: **Recognition of Syllables in Words**

Objective: To make students aware that words have one or more word parts called syllables and how to break up words into syllables to enhance their word attack skills.

Day 1: Record the following words on a chart: day, clog, hug, fish, bed. Have the students say and clap each word. How many times did you clap for each word? (one) How many vowels does each word contain? (one) Explain that a one syllable word contains only one vowel that is heard. Record these words on the chart: happy, rabbit, camel, music, pocket. Have the students clap and say each word. How many claps did each word receive? (2 claps) How many vowel sounds did you hear in each word? (two) Which vowel sounds did you hear in the word 'happy?' (short a; long e); rabbit (short a, short i); camel (short a, short e); music (long u, short i); pocket (short o, short e)

Activity Worksheet: Page 57 **A.** The students are to record the number of vowel sounds that are seen and heard in each word. **B.** The students are to record the number of vowel sounds heard in each word and the number of syllables. **Answer Key: A.** Column 1: leaf - 2, 1; boat - 2, 1; basket - 2, 2; factory - 3, 3; jerk - 1, 1; peas - 2, 1 Column 2: short - 1, 1; popcorn - 2, 2; fairy - 3, 2; farm - 1,1; garden - 2, 2; turnip - 2, 2 **B.** Column 1: happy - 2, 2; please - 1, 1; cricket - 2, 2; train - 1, 1; brush - 1, 1; slipper - 2, 2 Column 2: paint - 1, 1; cross - 1, 1; raindrop - 2, 2; skates - 1, 1; music - 2, 2; snowflakes - 2, 2

Day 2: Review the number of syllables and the number of vowel sounds heard in a word. Listen to each word that I say. How many syllables do you hear? Tell why. **Words:** 1. cricket (short i, e; 2 syllables) 2. branch (short a; 1 syllable) 3. cross (short o; 1 syllable) 4. brush (short u; 1 syllable) 5. rabbit (short a, i; 2 syllables) 6. oatmeal (long o, e; 2 syllables) 7. breeze (long e; 1 syllable) 8. turkey (short u; long e, 2 syllables)

Activity Worksheet: Page 58 The students are to record the number of syllables and the vowel sounds heard in each word. **Answer Key:** 1. (1) long e 2. (2) short i, short e 3. (2) short a, long e 4. (1) short a 5. (2) short i, short e 6. (1) long a 7. (2) short a, long e 8. (1) short o 9. (2) short o, long o 10. (2) short o, short e 11. (2) long a, long a 12. (1) long o

Day 3: On a chart record the following words: farm, fern, firm, form, fur. Discuss the words. What does each word contain? (one vowel sound) Circle the two letters that are making the vowel sound in each word. How many syllables are in each word? (1) Record the following words: turkey, garden, squirrel, rabbit, basket. How are these words different? (They have two vowels and two syllables.) Remind the students that a one syllable word has one vowel sound and a two syllable word has two vowel sounds heard.

Activity Worksheet: Page 59 The students are to circle the vowel sounds heard in each word and to record the number of syllables in each one on the line. **Answer Key:** Group 1: e, 1; a, y, 2; a, o, 2; a, 1; i, e, 2; e, 1; a, 1; o, o, 2; o, a, 2; a, 1; a, e, 2; o, o, 2 Group 2: e, 1; u, i, 2; e, 1; i, 1; a, a, 2; i, e, 2; i, e, e, 3; u, e, 2; a, u, a, 3; o, y, 2; o, 1; a, o, y, 3 Group 3: o, y, a, 3; o, a, 2; o, i, 2; i, e, 2; u, i, o, 3; u, 1; i, i, 2; i, 1; e, o, 2; a, 1; e, e, a, 3; a, 1

Day 4: On a chart record the following syllables: per, cor, tur, ner, squir, thun, pet, son, nip, rel, der, trum Have the students use the syllables to make the following words: person, trumpet, turnip, corner, squirrel, thunder

Activity Worksheet: Page 60 The students are to form words using the syllables in each box. **Answer Key:** Box A: myself, secret, bitten, ginger **B.** rabbit, hidden, canyon, trumpet **C.** dessert, turnip, carton, farmer **D.** lazy, bunny, create, teacher **E.** tender, supper, pantry, complete **F.** basket, chimney, lantern, pattern **G.** fifteen, carpet, monkey, finger **H.** complete, after, pony, painting

Day 5: Auditory and Visual Discrimination Test on Words With One to Three Syllables. Page 61 **Auditory Test: A.** The students are to circle the number of syllables in each word spoken by the teacher. Words: 1. gingerbread 2. booming 3. blow 4. newspaper 5. carving 6. purse 7. coming 8. Saturday 9. lightning 10. dangerous Answer Key" 1. (3) 2. (2) 3. (1) 4. (3) 5. (2) 6. (1) 7. (2) 8. (3) 9. (2) 10. (3)

Visual Discrimination Test: B. The students are to record the number of syllables seen in each word and then use each word in a sentence.
Answer Key: B. 1 (3) 2. (2) 3. (2) 4. (1) 5. (1) 6. (2) 7. (3) 8. (2) 9. (3) 10. (1) 11. (1) 12. (2) 13. (3) 14. (3) 15. (1) **C.** 1. strawberry 2. worm 3. nut 4. chalkboard 5. telephone 6. banana 7. grapes 8. pitchfork

Name: _____   Day 1 | Week 9

Words have different word parts called **syllables**. In each syllable there is usually a **long** or **short** vowel.

A. Say each word carefully. **Record** the number of vowels that you can **see** and the number of vowels that you can **hear** on the lines.

Words	Vowels Seen	Vowels Heard	Words	Vowels Seen	Vowels Heard
leaf	_____	_____	short	_____	_____
boat	_____	_____	popcorn	_____	_____
basket	_____	_____	fairy	_____	_____
factory	_____	_____	farm	_____	_____
jerk	_____	_____	garden	_____	_____
peas	_____	_____	turnip	_____	_____

B. *Remember this rule!*: A *one vowel* sound heard in a word makes it a *one syllable* word. *Two vowel* sounds heard in a word make it a *two syllable* word.

Record the number of **vowel sounds** heard in each word and the number of **syllables** each one has on the lines.

Words	Vowels Heard	Syllables	Words	Vowels Heard	Syllables
happy	_____	_____	paint	_____	_____
please	_____	_____	cross	_____	_____
cricket	_____	_____	raindrop	_____	_____
train	_____	_____	skates	_____	_____
brush	_____	_____	music	_____	_____
slipper	_____	_____	snowflake	_____	_____

Name: _____   Day 2 | Week 9

Remember: A one syllable word has one vowel sound that you can hear.

A two syllable word has two vowels that you can hear.

Record the number of syllables and vowel sounds heard in each word on the chart.

If you can hear two vowel sounds in a word, the word has two syllables.

Example: basket   2   short a, short e

Words	Syllables	Vowel Sounds Heard
1. street	_____	_____
2. cricket	_____	_____
3. frosty	_____	_____
4. strap	_____	_____
5. squirrel	_____	_____
6. skates	_____	_____
7. grassy	_____	_____
8. cross	_____	_____
9. popcorn	_____	_____
10. pocket	_____	_____
11. airplane	_____	_____
12. fork	_____	_____

Name: _____ Day 3 | Week 9

Don't forget these rules!

1. A word has **one syllable** if **one vowel** sound is heard.
2. A word has **two syllables** if **two vowel** sounds are heard.

Circle the vowels heard in each word and **record** the number of syllables in each one on the line.

Group 1	Group 2	Group 3
fresh ____	street ____	ponytail ____
grassy ____	music ____	snowflake ____
rainbow ____	please ____	robin ____
plant ____	fish ____	mitten ____
cricket ____	pancake ____	uniform ____
creep ____	kitten ____	mule ____
branch ____	gingerbread ____	icicle ____
bottom ____	thunder ____	thick ____
snowman ____	Saturday ____	elbow ____
tail ____	forty ____	chain ____
basket ____	short ____	elephant ____
photo ____	factory ____	harm ____

Name: _____ | Day 4 | Week 9 |

Match a syllable in the first column to a syllable in the second column in each box to make **four** words.

Record the words on the lines.

Let's make words with syllables!

A.
my	cret	_____
se	self	_____
bit	ger	_____
gin	ten	_____

E.
ten	per	_____
sup	plete	_____
pan	der	_____
com	try	_____

B.
rab	den	_____
hid	yon	_____
can	bit	_____
trum	pet	_____

F.
bas	tern	_____
chim	per	_____
lan	ket	_____
pat	ney	_____

C.
des	nip	_____
tur	mer	_____
car	sert	_____
far	ton	_____

G.
fif	key	_____
car	teen	_____
mon	ger	_____
fin	pet	_____

D.
la	ate	_____
bun	er	_____
cre	ny	_____
teach	zy	_____

H.
com	ny	_____
af	plete	_____
po	ing	_____
paint	ter	_____

Name: _____ Day 5 | Week 9

A. Auditory Test on the Recognition of Syllables

1. 1 2 3	2. 1 2 3	3. 1 2 3	4. 1 2 3	5. 1 2 3
6. 1 2 3	7. 1 2 3	8. 1 2 3	9. 1 2 3	10. 1 2 3

B. Visual Discrimination Test on the Recognition of Syllables

Record the number of syllables that you hear in each word on the line.

1. elephant _____
2. chalkboard _____
3. danger _____
4. fell _____
5. worm _____
6. children _____
7. telephone _____
8. pitchfork _____
9. strawberry _____
10. nut _____
11. grapes _____
12. corner _____
13. banana _____
14. yesterday _____
15. smile _____

C. Which of the above words match each riddle?

1. I am a red fruit that grows in June. _____
2. You often see me wiggling in dirt. _____
3. A squirrel loves to find one. _____
4. You can write or draw pictures on me. _____
5. You use me to talk to your friends. _____
6. I am a yellow fruit that grows in a bunch on a tree. _____
7. We are purple or green and grow on vines. _____
8. I am used to scoop up hay. _____

Week 10: **Recognition and Usage of 'R' Blends, 'L' Blends, and 'S' Blends**

Objective: To review the recognition and usage of 'R' blends, 'L' Blends and 'S' Blends in the initial position of words.

Day 1: Review the 'r' blends 'br, cr, dr, fr, gr, tr, pr, and wr.' Record the following words on a chart: branch, crayon, dream, frown, grass, tree, present, wrap. Have the students say the words. How does each word begin? (with an 'r' blend) Name the 'r' blends and make each sound. List them on the chart and have the students say each sound. **Listening Activity:** Which of these blends is heard at the beginning of each word that I am going to say? **Words:** fringe, dribble, tremble, prickly, wrinkle, grunt, bruise, crackle

Picture Key: Row 1: wrist, trumpet, present, grapes Row 2: frame, dragon, crab, braids

Activity Worksheet: Page 63 **A.** The students will record the name of each picture on the line. **B.** The sentences will be completed using the words in the Word Box. **Answer Key: A.** Row 1: wrist, trumpet, present, grapes Row 2: frame, dragon, crab, braids **B.** 1. trunk 2. fruit 3. drum 4. brush 5. crown 6. broom 7. crowd 8. proud

Day 2: Review the recognition of the 'l' blends 'bl, cl, fl, gl, pl, sl.' Record the following words on a chart: black, clock, flat, glad, plane, slap. Have the students say the words. Discuss the beginning sounds. How does each word begin? (with an 'l' blend) **Listening Activity:** Which of the 'l' blends is at the beginning of each word that I say. **Words:** flash, glance, platform, slug, clumsy, blister, glitter, pleasant, sleek, plaza, fluffy, clump, blower

Picture Key: Row 1: flag, block, globe, fly Row 2: slide, plant, cloud, glass

Activity Worksheet: Page 64 **A.** The students are to record the names of the pictures on the lines. **Answer Key:** Row 1: flag, block, globe, fly Row 2: slide, plant, cloud, glass **B.** The students will complete the sentences with the given words. **Answer Key:** 1. flames 2. glide 3. blindfold 4. closet 5. slice 6. plumber 7. flour 8. blender

Day 3: Review the 's' blends 'sl, st, sp, sm, sn, sk, str, spl, squ, sw, sc, scr, spr.' Record the two and three letter blends on a chart. Review the sounds that they make. Have the students locate the blend that they hear at the beginning of each of the following words: 1. squash 2. straw 3. scream 4. stars 5. splash 6. sweater 7. space 8. smile 9. stamp 10. slither 11. sprinkle 12. snack

Picture Key: Row 1: screw, scarecrow, snowman, swing Row 2: skates, sled, string, spoon Row 3: star, snake, store, snail Row 4: squirrel, stamp, sweater, strawberry Row 5: spool, spider, skunk, smoke

Activity Worksheet: Page: 65 The students will circle the blend heard in each picture. **Answer Key:** Row 1: scr, sc, sn, sw Row 2: sk, sl, str, sp Row 3: st, sn, st, sn Row 4: squ, st, sw, str Row 5: sp, sp, sk, sm

Day 4: Review the two and three letter 's' blends. Record the following blends on a chart: sc, sl, sm, sn, sp, st, sw, sk, str, scr, spl, spr, squ. Say one of the following words and have a student locate the blend heard at its beginning. **Words:** swarm, skinny, stork, scar, smear, sliver, snuggle, spend, split, snip, straw, scrub, splash, squint

Activity Worksheet: Page 66 The students will complete each sentence with the correct word. **Answer Key:** 1. sweep 2. splash 3. speech 4. snore 5. skip 6. scarf 7. slam 8. smack 9. swamp 10. storm 11. string 12. squeak

Day 5: Auditory and Visual Discrimination Test on the Two and Three Letter 'S, L, and R' Blends
Auditory Test: Page 67 The students are to record the 's' blend heard at the beginning of each word said by the teacher. **Words:** 1. split 2. sneeze 3. sponge 4. swollen 5. scream 6. smack 7. scar 8. sloppy 9. skeleton 10. string 11. squint 12. sprout **Answer Key:** 1. spl 2. sn 3. sp 4. sw 5. scr 6. sm 7. sc 8. sl 9. sk 10. str 11. squ 12. spr

Visual Discrimination Test: The students will select the correct word for each sentence. **Answer Key:** 1. scraps, floor 2. scarecrow, clothes, straw 3. stars, sparkle, sky 4. storm, flashed 5. clown, floppy, black 6. truck, drove 7. flames, spreading 8. squirrel, trunk, tree

Name: _____   Day 1 | Week 10

'R' Blends
br, cr, dr, fr, gr, pr, tr, wr

Remember: A **blend** is a sound made of two consonants found at the beginning of a word.

Some blends belong to the 'r' blend family.

They are **br**, **cr**, **dr**, **fr**, **gr**, **pr**, **tr**, **wr**.

A. Record the name of each picture on the line.

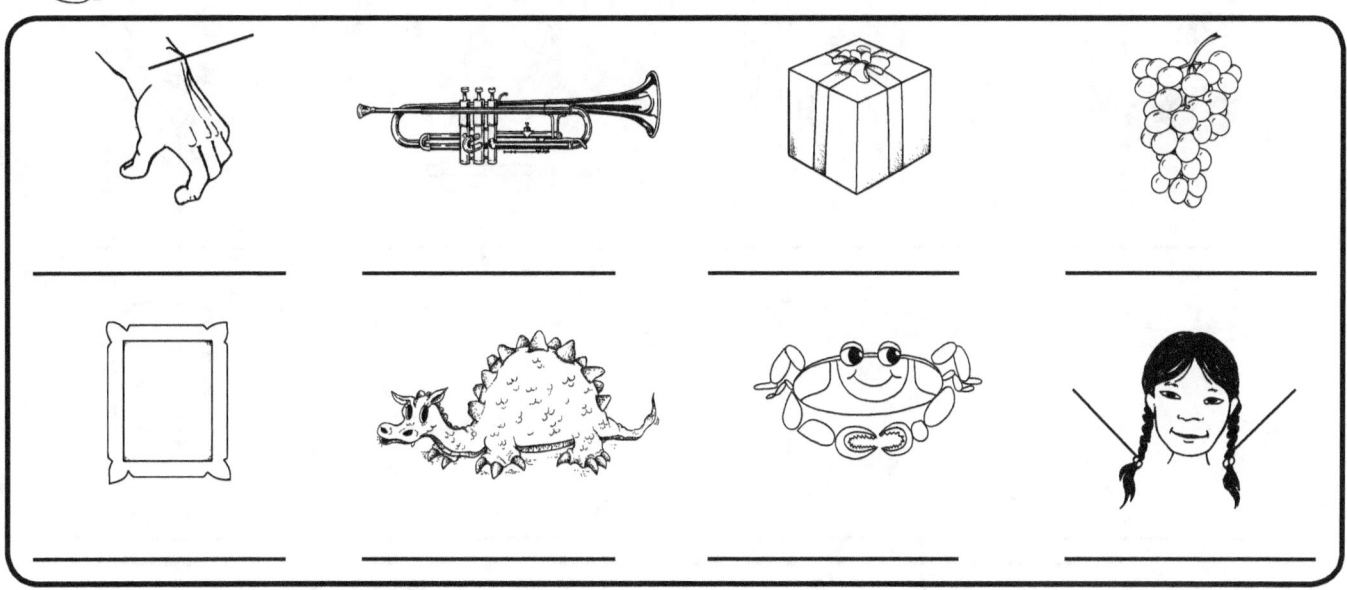

B. Use the words in the Word Box to complete each sentence.

Word Box
fruit   trunk   drum   proud   crown   crowd   brush   broom

1. Jeff packed all of his toys in a big _____.

2. The glass bowl on the table was full of many kinds of _____.

3. A small boy played the biggest _____ in the marching band.

4. Did you remember to _____ your teeth this morning

5. The queen wore a _____ when she spoke to her people.

6. Use the _____ to sweep the dirt off the sidewalk.

7. The _____ cheered loudly when their team won the game.

8. I was very _____ of my good report card.

Name: _____ Day 2 | Week 10

Some words begin with an 'l' blend.

The 'l' blends are **bl, cl, fl, gl, pl, sl**.

Examples: **bl**ack, **cl**oud, **fl**at, **gl**ass, **pl**ane, **sl**ide

A. Record the name of each picture on the line.

_____ _____ _____ _____

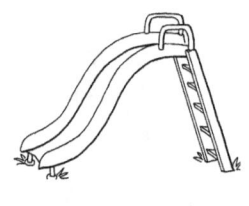   

_____ _____ _____ _____

B. Use the words in the Word Box to complete the sentences.

Word Box
flames blindfold closet slice plumber glide flour blender

1. The _____, of the fire that we made, kept us warm at night.

2. We watched the plane _____ when it landed on the water in the lake.

3. We had to wear a _____ in one of the games that we played at the party.

4. We hung our coats in the big hall _____.

5. I ate the biggest _____ of the chocolate cake.

6. A _____ came to my house to fix the tap that was leaking.

7. My mother used, white _____, sugar and chocolate chips to make some cookies.

8. We made strawberry milkshakes with a _____.

Name: _____   Day 3 | Week 10

sc sl sm st
sk sw str spl
squ scr sn sp
spr

Some words begin with sounds called **'s' blends**.

Some of these blends have **two** or three letters and are found at the beginning of words.

Examples: scare, sleep, smile, stop, skin, sweep, string, splash, square, scrub, snap, spin, spray

Circle the 's' blend heard at the **beginning** of each picture.

sp scr sm	sn scr sc	sm sn sp	spl spr sw
sn sk squ	sl sk spl	spr str scr	spr sp st
sn sl st	st sn sm	sp str st	spl sm sn
spl str squ	sp st sm	sw scr spl	scr spr str
spr sp sn	sm sp sl	sc sk st	sm sn sl

65

Name: _____   Day 4 | Week 10

Many words begin with **two** and **three** letter 's' blends.

Use your word attack skills to find the word missing from from each sentence in the Word Box.

Record the missing word on the line in each one.

Word Box

| squeak | storm | slam | skip | snore | splash |
| string | swamp | smack | scarf | speech | sweep |

1. You can _____ the dirty floor with this broom.

2. The children like to _____ each other in the lake.

3. We listened to the _____ made by Canada's Prime Minister.

4. We heard our grandfather _____ while he was sleeping.

5. Some girls like to play games or _____ at recess.

6. I had to wear a _____ over my mouth and nose because it was so cold outside.

7. Do not _____ the door when you leave the house.

8. I heard a fish _____ its tail on the top of the water.

9. A _____ is a very wet and muddy place.

10. I heard thunder and saw lightning during the _____.

11. I tied a long _____ to my kite so it would fly high in the sky.

12. The big wheels on the old wagon _____ when they move.

Name: _____   Day 5 | Week 10

A. Auditory Test on 'R', 'L' and 'S' Blends

1. _____	2. _____	3. _____	4. _____
5. _____	6. _____	7. _____	8. _____
9. _____	10. _____	11. _____	12. _____

B. Visual Discrimination Test on 'R, L, and S Blends'

tree	floor	floppy	sky	spreading
drove	squirrel	clothes	stars	flashed
storm	flames	trunk	scraps	straw
sparkle	black	truck	clown	scarecrow

1. Please pick up the _____ of paper that are on the _____.

2. The _____ was made out of old _____ and _____.

3. The _____ at night _____ in the dark _____.

4. During the _____ the lightning _____ and the thunder roared.

5. The circus _____ wore big _____ shoes and a _____ hat

6. The delivery man hopped into his _____ and _____ away.

7. The _____ of the forest fire were _____ quickly through the the forest.

8. The _____ ran up the _____ of the _____ to hide the nut.

SSR1142 ISBN: 9781771586887   67   © On The Mark Press

Week 11: Recognition of 'ar, or, ir, ur and er' in Words

Objective: To reinforce the recognition and usage of 'ar, or, er, ur, and ir' in words.

Day 1: At the top of a chart, record the r - controlled sounds 'ar, er, ir, or, and ur.' Under the sounds record the following unfinished words. **Words:** 1. b __ __ k 2. st __ __ 3. d __ __ t 4. c __ __ n 5. c __ __ l 6. b __ __ n 7. p __ __ ch 8. f __ __ m 9. c __ __ k 10. st __ __ m **Possible Answers:** 1. bark 2. star, stir 3. dirt, dart 4. corn 5. curl 6. born, barn, burn 7. porch, perch, parch 8. farm, form, firm 9. cork 10. storm

Picture Key: Row 1: tiger, horn, star, bird Row 2: church, letter, turtle, fork

Activity Worksheet: Page 69 **A.** The students are to spell the name of each picture correctly on the line. **B.** The students are to complete the words with the correct 'r' controlled sound. **Answer Key: A.** Row 1: tiger, horn, star, bird Row 2: church, letter, turtle, fork **B.** Box 1: circle, letter, scarf, corn, jerk, bird, horn, jar Box 2: skirt, hard, turtle, sparkle, ladder, third, turkey, mother Box 3: purse, yard, paper, barn, curl, farm, dark, storm Box 4: purple, hurt, yarn, slipper, fire, burn, nurse, mark

Day 2: On a chart record 'ar, er, ir, or, ur.' Under the sounds record the following word parts: 1. f(ar), f(ur), f(ir), f(or) 2. b(ir)d 3. c(or)k 4. st(ar), st(ir) 5. b(ar)n, b(ur)n, b(or)n 6. d(ar)k 7. sp(ar)kle 8. st(ar)e, st(or)e Have the students choose the correct 'r' sound to complete each word or groups of words.

Activity Worksheet: Page 70 The students are to complete each sentence with the correct word in the Word Box. **Answer Key:** 1. horn 2. wore, skirt 3. fur, thicker 4. purple, slippers 5. hurt, car, father 6. church, morning 7. stars, sparkle, dark 8. over, garden 9. sparkle, winter 10. nurse, better

Day 3: On a chart record 'ar, er, ir, or, and ur.' Under the sounds record the following word parts: 1. f(ar), f(ir), f(ur), f(or) 2. b(ir)d 3. c(or)k 4. st(ar), st(ir) 5. b(ar)n, b(ur)n, b(or)n 6. d(ar)k 7. sp(ar)kle 8. st(or)e, st(ar)e Have the students choose the correct 'r' sound to complete each word or groups of words.

Activity Worksheet: Page 71 **A.** The students are to underline the words in each sentence that contain 'ar, er, or, ir, ur.' **B.** The students are to classify the words in the sentences under the sounds. **Answer Key: ar** - farmer's, market, warm, bar, large **er** - mother, thicker, winter, finger, water, covered, feathers, very, her **ur** - during, turkey, turtle, surf, burst **ir**- whirl, girl, girl's thirsty, dirty, circus **or** - storm, doctor, for, corn, horse

Day 4: On a chart record the following words with missing vowel + 'r' sounds: 1. sp<u>ur</u>s 2. f<u>or</u>k 3. thund<u>er</u> 4. c<u>ar</u>d, c<u>or</u>d 5. sh<u>ir</u>t, sh<u>or</u>t 6. f<u>ar</u>m, f<u>ir</u>m, f<u>or</u>m 7. sh<u>ir</u>t, sh<u>or</u>t 8. b<u>or</u>n, b<u>ur</u>n, b<u>ar</u>n 9. t<u>or</u>n, t<u>ur</u>n 10. d<u>ir</u>t, d<u>ar</u>t

Activity Worksheet: Page 72 The students will complete the words in the sentences with the vowel + 'r' sounds. **Answer Key:** 1. mother, bird, her, for 2. corn 3. fork, supper 4. farm, horses, barn 5. wore, shirt, shorts 6. purse, church 7. score, soccer 8. mother, thunder, during, storm 9. During, winter, dark, short 10. birthday, party

Day 5: Auditory Test on Vowel + 'R' Blends Page 73
The students will circle the sound heard in each word spoken by the teacher. **Words:** 1. turkey 2. organ 3. danger 4. spark 5. dirty 6. garden 7. over 8. sore 9. purple 10. skirt **Answer Key:** 1. ur 2. or 3. er 4. ar 5. ir 6. ar 7. er 8. or 9. ur 10. ir

Visual Discrimination Test: The students will complete each sentence with a word from the Word Box. **Answer Key:** 1. stars, sparkle, dark 2. garden, garter, flowers 3. church, organ 4. girl, skirt, dirty 5. clover, hunter 6. warm, shower 7. butter, churn 8. farm, barn, winter

Name: _____   Day 1 | Week 11

ar or ir
ur er

In some words the letter 'r' controls the sound made by its vowel partner.

Examples: star, stir, store, hurt, letter

A. Spell the name of each picture on the line

_____   _____   _____   _____

_____   _____   _____   _____

B. Complete each word with the correct 'r' sound

c ___ ___ cle	sk ___ ___ t	p ___ ___ se	p ___ ___ ple
lett ___ ___	h ___ ___ d	y ___ ___ d	h ___ ___ t
sc ___ ___ f	t ___ ___ tle	pap ___ ___	y ___ ___ n
c ___ ___ n	sp ___ ___ kle	b ___ ___ n	slipp ___ ___
j ___ k	ladd ___ ___	c ___ l	f ___ e
b ___ d	th ___ ___ d	f ___ m	b ___ ___ n
h ___ n	t ___ ___ key	d ___ k	n ___ se
j ___ ___	moth ___ ___	st ___ m	m ___ k

Name: _____   Day 2 | Week 11

The sounds 'ar, er, ir, or, ur' are found in many words.
Use the words in the Word Box to **complete** each sentence.

Word Box

nurse	purple	over	wore	father
fur	church	horn	hurt	sparkle
car	better	dark	stars	skirt
garden	morning	slippers	winter	thicker

1. Jack can play a big _____ called a tuba.

2. Marie _____ a blue _____ and a white blouse to school.

3. An animal's _____ gets _____ in the winter.

4. Put on your _____ _____ if your feet are cold.

5. David was not _____ in the _____ accident with his _____.

6. The _____ bell rang loudly every Sunday _____.

7. _____ _____ in the _____ sky at night.

8. The wind blew the leaves all _____ the _____.

9. The sun makes the snow _____ in the _____.

10. A _____ helps sick people get _____.

Name: _____ Day 3 | Week 11

Do you remember the vowels a,e,i,o,u?

Remember the vowels 'a, e, i, o, u' and the consonant 'r' join hands to make one sound.

Examples: h**ar**d, h**er**d, f**ir**, f**or**, f**ur**

A. Circle the words in the sentences that contain '**ar**, **er**, **ir**, **or**, and **ur**.

1. My mother likes to shop at a farmer's market to buy corn.

2. The leaves began to whirl about in the wind during the storm.

3. Animals get thicker coats to keep them warm during the winter.

4. The doctor looked at the cut on the girl's finger.

5. The girl hung by her knees on the bar.

6. The boy was thirsty and drank lots of water.

7. The big turkey was covered with black and white feathers.

8. The large turtle walked into the ocean surf and swam away.

9. The horse rolled in the mud and got very dirty.

10. At the circus the clowns like to burst big balloons.

B. Record the words from the sentences that contain 'ar, or, ir, ur, er'

ar	er	ur	ir	or
___	___	___	___	___
___	___	___	___	___
___	___	___	___	___
___	___	___	___	___
___	___	___	___	___

Name: _____ Day 4 | Week 11

How well can you spell words that have 'ar, er, ir, or, ur' inside or at the end of them?

Remember these sounds!
ar, er, ir, or, ur

Examples: star   letter   first   horn   burn

Complete the word in the sentences using these sounds.

1. A moth____ b____d does not leave h____ nest f____ a long time.

2. The chickens ate all of the c____n in the box.

3. I use a f____k and a knife when I eat my supp____.

4. At the f____m I saw h____ses eating hay in the b____n.

5. I w____e a blue sh____t with my white sh____ts to school.

6. I found a lady's p____se outside of our ch____ch.

7. The sc____e of the socc____ game was very high.

8. My moth____ does not like to hear the thund____ d____ing a st____m.

9. D____ing the wint____ some days in Iqaluit are d____k and sh____t.

10. I went to my best friends b____thday p____ty.

Name: _____   Day 5 | Week 11

A. Auditory Discrimination Test on 'ar, er, ir, or, ur'

1. ar er ur	2. or ar ur	3. ir er or	4. er ar ir	5. ar ir or
6. or ir ar	7. ir ur er	8. ar or ir	9. or er ur	10. ar ir or

B. Visual Discrimination Test on 'ar, er, ir, or, ur'

Word Box

barn	hunter	farm	churn	warm
girl	skirt	shower	butter	organ
clover	dirty	church	garden	flowers
garter	stars	sparkle	dark	winter

1. At night _____ twinkle and _____ in the _____ sky.

2. In our _____ lives a _____ snake who hides in the _____.

3. The music in the _____ came from an old _____.

4. The little _____ fell in a puddle and got her _____ _____.

5. The rabbit enjoyed eating the _____ until it saw the _____.

6. I like to have a _____ _____ before I go to bed.

7. A long time ago people in Canada made their _____ in a _____.

8. On a _____ animals are kept in a _____ in the _____.

SSR1142 ISBN: 9781771586887

Week 12: Using Suffixes 'ed, ing, es, er, est

Objective: To teach the meaning of a root word that is a verb or action word and how it can be changed to mean a) its happening (present tense); b) it has happened (past tense), and c) it will happen (future tense) by adding the suffixes 's, ed, and ing' to a root word.

Day 1: On a chart record the following action words: play, plays, played, playing. Under the words record the following sentences: 1. Come outside and play with me. (present) 2. He plays with his dog every day. (present) 3. The children played a silly game. (past) 4. He will play with you tomorrow. (future) Explain to your students that the word '**play**' is an **action** word called a **verb**. An action word tells when something is happening, when something has happened, or when something will happen in the future or later on.

Activity Worksheet: Page 75 **A.** The students will record each verb with the suffixes 's, ed, ing'. **B.** The students will record the root word for each of the given words. **Answer Key: A.** 1. helps, helped, helping 2. cooks, cooked, cooking 3. opens, opened, opening 4. jumps, jumped, jumping 5. starts, started, starting 6. learns, learned, learning 7. cleans, cleaned, cleaning 8. picks, picked, picking **B.** 1. draw 2. walk 3. open 4. cook 5. dress 6. burn 7. hop 8. help 9. talk 10. listen 11. work 12. sleep 13. look 14. row

Day 2: Review adding the suffixes 'es, ed, ing, er, and est' to words ending with an 'e'. Record the following groups of words on a chart. Words: 1. bike, bikes, biked, biking 2. rake, rakes, raked, raking 3. fine, finer, finest 4. cute, cuter, cutest 5. take, taking 6. shine, shining 7. cute, cuter, cutest 5. make, making 6. ride, riding 7. hide, hiding 8. smile, smiling. Have the students add the correct suffixes to each word. Suffixes: s, es, ed, ing, er, est. Review the rule with your students.

Activity Worksheet: Page: 76 **A.** The students are to complete each sentence by adding a suffix to the word in the brackets. **B.** The students are to circle the word in each sentence that has a suffix and record its root word on the line. **Answer Key: A.** 1. raised 2. lived 3. glued 4. skating 5. lives 6. invited 7. cutest 8. dancer **B.** 1. baked, bake 2. skates, skate 3. biggest, big 4. smallest, small 5. riding, ride 6. saving, save 7. smiled, smile

Day 3: Discuss the sufixes 'es, er, and est' that are added to the end of a root word that ends with the vowel 'e' that is silent. Explain that when a word ends with the vowel 'e', the vowel is dropped and a suffix that begins with a vowel is added. Examples: care, cares, cared, caring. Have the students form new words using the suffixes 'es, ed, ing.' On a chart record the following words and beside each one have the students write each word with the suffix correctly. Words: rake rakes, raked, raking 2. chase, chases, chased, chasing 3. smile, smiles, smiled, smiling 4. skate, skates, skated, skating

Activity Worksheet: Page 77 **A.** The students are to record the given word at the end of each sentence with the correct suffix in it. **B.** The students are to circle the word in each sentence that ends with a suffix and then print the root word on the line at the end of it. **Answer Key: A.** 1. raised 2. lived 3. glued 4. skating 5. lives 6. invited 7. cutest 8. dancer **B.** 1. baked 2. skates 3. biggest 4. smallest 5. riding 6. saving 7. ripped, climbed

Day 4: Review adding the suffixes '**s**, **es**, **ed**, **ing**, **er**, and **est**' to words that end with a consonant or a vowel. Remind them of the rule about root words that end with a silent 'e'. On a chart list the following suffixes across the top: s, ed, ing, er, est. Under the suffixes in a list record the following words and have the students add any of the following suffixes 'e, es, ed, ing, er, est to the end of each one. **Words:** 1. toy __ 2. fine__ 3. play__ 4. clean __ 5. spell __ 6. neat __ 7. rake 8. tail __ 9. loud __ 10. hike __

Activity Worksheet: Page 78 **A.** The students are to add the suffixes 's, ed, and ing' to words. **B.** The students are to make new words by adding the suffixes 'er' and 'est' to root words. **C.** Students are to record the root word for each given word. **Answer Key: A.** 1. bikes, biked, biking 2. mails, mailed, mailing 3. jumps, jumped, jumping 4. sails, sailed, sailing 5. rains, rained, raining 6. rakes, raked, raking **B.** 1. larger, largest 2. older, oldest 3. smaller, smallest 4. colder, coldest 5. lighter, lightest **C.** 1. pile 2. make 3. play 4. leave 5. smile 6. shine

Day 5: A. Auditory Test on the Suffixes 's, es, ed, ing, er, est: Page 79 The students are to circle the suffix that is heard at the end of each word said by the teacher. Words: 1. sickest 2. started 3. makes 4. cleaner 5. caps 6. walking 7. quicker 8. hikes. **A. Answer Key:** 1. est 2. ed 3. es 4. er 5. s 6. ing 7. er 8. s

B. Visual Discrimination Test on Suffixes 's, es, ed, ing, er, est': The students are to add the correct suffix to each word and to record it in the sentence. **Answer Key: B.** 1. taking 2. hiked 3. rakes 4. coldest 5. shining 6. older 7. hiding 8. tall **C.** 1. hide 2. bake 3. smile 4. chase 5. cute 6. thick

Name: _____   Day 1 | Week 12

The words '*jump, play,* and *laugh*' are called **root words** and **action** words.

Sometimes the suffixes '**e**, **ed**, and **ing**' are added to the ends of root words that are action words.

Examples: jump**s**, jump**ed**, jump**ing**

A. Make new words by adding the suffixes **s**, **ed**, and **ing** to each root word.

Word	s	ed	ing
1. help	_____	_____	_____
2. cook	_____	_____	_____
3. open	_____	_____	_____
4. jump	_____	_____	_____
5. start	_____	_____	_____
6. learn	_____	_____	_____
7. clean	_____	_____	_____
8. pick	_____	_____	_____

B. The suffixes '**s, ed, and ing**' are often added to a **root word**. Record the root word on the line for each of the words below.

1. drawing	_____	8. helping	_____
2. walked	_____	9. talks	_____
3. opens	_____	10. listened	_____
4. cooking	_____	11. working	_____
5. dressing	_____	12. sleeps	_____
6. burned	_____	13. looked	_____
7. hops	_____	14. rowing	_____

Name: _____   Day 2 | Week 12

The groups of letters '**es**, **ed**, **ing**, **er** and **est**' are called '**suffixes**.'

They are often added to the **ends** of **root words**.

Examples: jump**ed**   open**ing**   cook**s**   roll**er**   tall**est**

Rule: If a word ends with a **silent** '**e**', you **drop** the '**e**' before adding a suffix that begins with a **vowel**.

Examples: fine   finer   finest ;   chase   chases   chasing   chased

A. Complete each sentence by adding the correct **suffix** to the word in the brackets.

1. The caretaker _____ Canada's flag on the flagpole outside the school. (raise)

2. The grey squirrel _____ in a hole in the old oak tree. (live)

3. We _____ some photos in a book about our family. (glue)

4. We went _____ on the pond today. (skate)

5. Who _____ in that old scary house. (live)

6. We were _____ to Jeff's birthday party. (invite)

7. Who has the _____ puppy for a pet? (cute)

8. My sister is a very good _____. (dance)

B. **Circle** the word in each sentence that has a suffix and **print** its root word on the line.

1. My mother baked an apple pie today.   _____

2. I have new skates to wear at the rink.   _____

3. Tony ate the biggest apple in the bowl.   _____

4. My kitten is the smallest one in the basket.   _____

5. Who is riding the big black horse in the parade.   _____

6. I am saving money in my bank for a new bike.   _____

7. Janet smiled when she won first prize.   _____

Name: _____ Day 3 | Week 12

Suffixes are often added to the **ends** of words. The suffixes are '**s**, **es**, **ed**, **ing**, **er**, and **est**.'

Rule: If a word ends with a **silent 'e,'** you drop the '**e**' before before **adding** a suffix that begins with a vowel.

A. **Complete** each sentence by adding the correct **suffix** to the words in the brackets.

1. The school's caretaker _____ Canada's flag on the flagpole every morning. (raise)

2. The grey squirrel _____ in a hole in the oak tree. (live)

3. We _____ some photos in a book about our family. (glue)

4. We went _____ on the pond today. (skate)

5. Who _____ in that old, spooky house. (live)

6. We were _____ to Jeff's birthday party. (invite)

7. Who has the _____ little puppy? (cute)

8. My sister is a very good ballet _____. (dance)

B. **Circle** the word in each sentence that has a suffix and **print** its root word on the line at the end of it.

1. My mother baked an apple pie today. (_____)

2. I have new skates to wear at the rink. (_____)

3. Tony ate the biggest apple in the bowl. (_____)

4. My kitten is the smallest one in the basket. (_____)

5. Who is riding the big, black horse? (_____)

6. I am saving money in my piggy bank. (_____)

7. Janet ripped her pants on a nail when she climbed the fence. (_____) (_____)

Name: _____   Day 4 | Week 12

Remember: When a word ends with a **silent 'e'**, the 'e' is dropped **before** adding a suffix that begins with a **vowel**.

Examples: store   stores   stored   storing
hope   hopes   hoped   hoping

A. Make new words by adding the suffixes '**es, ed**, and **ing**.'

Words	s	ed	ing
1. bike	_____	_____	_____
2. mail	_____	_____	_____
3. jump	_____	_____	_____
4. sail	_____	_____	_____
5. rain	_____	_____	_____
6. rake	_____	_____	_____

B. Make new words by adding the suffixes '**er**' and '**est**.'

Words	er	est
1. large	_____	_____
2. old	_____	_____
3. small	_____	_____
4. cold	_____	_____
5. light	_____	_____

C. Record the **root word** for each of the words below on the line.

1. piled _____   4. leaving _____
2. makes _____   5. smiling _____
3. playing _____   6. shining _____

Name: _____   Day 5 | Week 12

A. Auditory Test on the Suffixes 's, es, ed, ing, er, est'

1. es est er	2. es ed er	3. ed ing s	4. er est es
5. es s ing	6. ing ed est	7. est s er	8. er s est

B. Visual Discrimination Test on Suffixes 's, es, ed, ing, er, est'

1. I am _____ my dog for a walk. (take)

2. We _____ up and down hills and walked through forests. (hike)

3. Every autumn Tommy _____ the leaves into piles. (rake)

4. This must be the _____ day that we have had this winter. (cold)

5. The sun is _____ brightly today. (shine)

6. My sister is _____ than me. (old)

7. Where do you think the fox is _____. (hide)

8. My brother is _____ than me. (tall)

C. Record the **root word** for each of the following words.

1. hiding _____   4. chases _____

2. bakes   _____   5. cutest _____

3. smiling _____   6. thicker _____

Week 13: Suffixes 'ed, ing, er, est, ly, ness, ful, less

Objective: To make students aware of the rules that apply to certain words when adding suffixes.

Day 1: Teach the following suffix rule: When a word ends with a silent 'e', drop the 'e' before adding a suffix that begins with a vowel. On a chart record the following groups of words: 1. hikes, hiked, hiking 2. skates, skated, skating 3. bakes, baked, baking 4. cares, cared, caring. Discuss the words. Record the root word for each one: 1. hike 2. skate 3. bake 4. care Have the students note the change made in each root word when the suffixes were added. Record the following words on the chart: 1. finer, finest 2. cuter, cutest 4. riper, ripest 5. wiser, wisest. Record the root word for each one. 1. fine 2. cute 3. ripe 4. wise Have the students note that the rule applies when adding 'er' and 'est'

Activity Worksheet: Page 81 **A.** The students are to make new words by adding the suffixes 'es, ed, ing.' **B.** The students are to make new words by adding the suffixes 'er' and 'est'. **C.** The students are to record the root word for each given word. **Answer Key: A.** 1. bikes, biked, biking 2. likes, liked, liking 3. rakes, raked, raking 4. skates, skated, skating **B.** 1. larger, largest 2. cuter, cutest 3. riper, ripest 4. finer, finest **C.** 1. close 2. bare 3. tie 4. lie 5. smile 6. hide 7. close 8. use

Day 2: Review adding suffixes 'es, ed, ing, er, est to words ending in 'e'. On a chart record the following words in a column: lie, kiss, bake, hate, please. Have the students add the suffixes 'es, ing, and ed' to each one. Remind them about the rules for adding suffixes. Record these words on the chart: cold, small, green, deep. Have the students add the suffixes 'er' and 'est' to each one.

Activity Worksheet: Page 82 **A.** The students are to make new words by adding the suffixes to root words. **B.** The students are to use the suffixes 'ful' and 'less' to create new words. **C.** The students are to record the root words. **Answer Key: A.** 1. quicker, quickest, quickly 2. louder, loudest, loudly 3. softer, softest, softly 4. harder, hardest, hardly 5. sicker, sickest, sickly **B.** 1. helpful, helpless 2. careful, careless 3. thankful, thankless 4. fearful, fearless 5. painful, painless 6. hopeful, hopeless 7. thoughtful, thoughtless 8. harmful, harmless **C.** 1. thank 2. help 3. blind 4. spoon 5. silent 6. quiet 7. quick 8. pain 9. glad 10. harm 11. neat 12. soft 13. fast 14. kind

Day 3: Discuss adding the suffixes 'es, ed, ing, er, est' to words ending with the letter 'e'. On a chart record the following groups of words in a column down it. **Words:** 1. rake 2. hike 3. chase 4. please. Beside each word have the students add the suffixes 'es, ed, and ing'. Review the suffix rule: When a word ends with a silent 'e', you are to drop the 'e' before adding a suffix that begins with a vowel. Record this group of words on the chart. Have the students add the suffixes 'er' and 'est'. **Words:** small, sick, near, cute, fine

Activity Worksheet: Page 83 **A.** The students are to add a suffix to a word in the word box so it will fit in the sentence. **B.** The students are to circle the word in the sentence that has a suffix and print its root word on the line at the end of it. **Answer Key: A.** 1. greener 2. fired 3. piles 4. skating 5. taller 6. hated 7. biggest **B.** 1. skates, skate 2. biggest, big 3. baked, bake 4. brushing, brush 5. laughing, laugh 6. loved, love 7. hiding, hide

Day 4: On a chart, record the following groups of words: 1. bat, bats, batted, batting 2. tag, tags, tagged, tagging 3. rob, robs, robbed, robbing 4. pin, pins, pinned, pinning 5. sob, sobs, sobbed, sobbing Have the students read aloud each group of words. Have them note how the end of each word is changed. Discuss the vowel sound heard in each group. (short vowels heard) Discuss how each root word in each group ends. (with one consonant) What happens when a suffix is added that has a vowel. (The final consonant is doubled before adding a suffix that begins with a vowel.) Record the following words on the chart: big, fat, cold, hot. Add 'er' and 'est' to each one. Have the students note the word 'cold' does not end with a single consonant and the last letter is not doubled when you add 'er' or 'est.'

Activity Worksheet: Page 84 **A.** The students are to circle root words that end with a single consonant and underline those that end with a double consonant. **B.** The students are to add the suffixes 'er' and 'est' to each word. **C.** The students are to record the root word for each given word. **Answer Key: A.** <u>Circled Words:</u> hop, drop, big, hot, beg, slap <u>Underlined Words:</u> jump, buck, spell, cold **B.** <u>Sentences:</u> 1. hottest 2. bucked 3. hopping 4. slapped 5. begged 6. spells 7. jumped 8. drops **C.** 1. richer, richest 2. brighter, brightest 3. lighter, lighest 4. fatter, fattest 5. hotter, hottest 6. bigger, biggest **D.** 1. tap 2. rob 3. scrub 4. skip 5. bake 6. smile 7. run 8. tall

Day 5: A. Auditory Test on the Sufixes 's, es, ed, ing, er, est, ly, ness, ful, less Page 85 The students will circle the suffix in each box heard at the end of each word spoken by the teacher. **Words:** 1. jumps 2. sickest 3. toys 4. careless 5. buying 6. smaller 7. kindly 8. kindest 9. ringing 10. hopeful **Answer Key:** 1. s 2. est 3. s 4. less 5. ing 6. er 7. ly 8. est 9. ing 10. ful

B. Visual Discrimination Test on the Suffixes 's, es, ed, ing, er, est, ly, ness, ful, less': The students will complete the sentences by adding the correct suffix to the word in the brackets. **Answer Key:** 1. lonely 2. harmful 3. homeless 4. hiking 5. bigger 6. largest 7. makes 8. smiles 9. neatest 10. tapped

SSR1142 ISBN: 9781771586887 80 © On The Mark Press

Name: _____   Day 1 | Week 13

Remember this rule: When a word ends with a silent '**e**', drop the '**e**' before adding a **suffix** that begins with a **vowel**.

Examples: smile   smiles   smiled   smiling

A. Make new words by adding the suffixes '**es**, **ed**, and **ing**'.

Words	es	ed	ing
1. bike	_____	_____	_____
2. like	_____	_____	_____
3. rake	_____	_____	_____
4. skate	_____	_____	_____

B. Make new words by adding the suffixes '**er**' and '**est**'.

Words	er	est
1. large	_____	_____
2. cute	_____	_____
3. ripe	_____	_____
4. fine	_____	_____

C. Record the **root word** for each of the following words.

1. closest _____
2. barest _____
3. tied _____
4. lies _____

5. smiles _____
6. hiding _____
7. closed _____
8. used _____

Name: _____ Day 2 | Week 13

There are other **suffixes** that can be added to **root words**.

They are **ly**, **ness**, **ful** and **less**.

Examples: careless   careful   kindly   kindness

A. Make new words by adding the suffixes '**er**, **est**, **ly** and **ness**'

1. quick _____ _____ _____
2. loud _____ _____ _____
3. soft _____ _____ _____
4. hard _____ _____ _____
5. sick _____ _____ _____

B. Add the suffixes '**ful**' and '**less**' to create new words.

1. help _____   help _____   5. pain _____   pain _____
2. care _____   care _____   6. hope _____   hope _____
3. thank _____ thank _____ 7. thought _____ thoughtless _____
4. fear _____   fear _____   8. harm _____   harm _____

C. Record the **root word** for each of the following words.

1. thankful _____   8. painful _____
2. helpless _____   9. gladly _____
3. blindness _____   10. harmful _____
4. spoonful _____   11. neatly _____
5. silently _____   12. softness _____
6. quietly _____   13. fastest _____
7. quickest _____   14. kindness _____

Name: _____   Day 3 | Week 13

Don't forget this rule!

When a **word** ends with a **silent 'e'**, you must drop the 'e' before adding a **suffix** that begins with a **vowel**.

A. Add the correct **suffix** to a word in the box and **print** it in one of the sentences.

> hate   tall   pile   fire   big   skate   green

1. The rain made the grass on the lawn _____.

2. The hunter _____ his gun and killed the angry bear.

3. The children raked the leaves into three big _____.

4. The three children enjoyed _____ on the big pond.

5. Tony is _____ than his older brother and sister.

6. Tammy _____ cleaning up her bedroom.

7. The _____ horse pulled the heavy wagon all by itself.

B. Circle each word in the sentences that has a **suffix** and print its **root word** on the line.

1. Maggie has a new pair of hockey skates. _____

2. Johnny ate the biggest apple in the basket. _____

3. My mother baked a chocolate cake for the party. _____

4. Tommy was brushing his new pony in the barn. _____

5. Everyone was laughing at the silly clown on a bicycle. _____

6. Quincy loved to play with his red and white ball. _____

7. Billy was hiding behind a big maple tree. _____

Name: _____   Day 4 | Week 13

Remember to use this rule!

> When a word ends with **one** consonant after a **short** vowel sound, you usually **double** the consonant before **adding** a suffix that begins with a vowel.

Examples: hop hops hop**ped** hop**ping**

A. In the box, **circle** the root words that end with a **single** consonant and **underline** the root words that end with a **double** consonant.

jump	hop	buck	drop	big
hot	beg	spell	slap	cold

B. Complete each sentence with a **root word** from the box by adding one of the following suffixes: **es, s, ed, ing, er, est**

1. Today was the _____ day this summer in Canada.
2. The horses at the Calgary Stampede _____ off many riders.
3. The little rabbit went _____ into the woods when it saw the fox.
4. The angry boy _____ his hand on the closed door.
5. The poor man sat outside the store and _____ for money.
6. The witch like to cast funny _____ to make people laugh.
7. The old black dog carefully _____ over the fence.
8. _____ of water ran down the glass in the window.

C. Add the suffixes 'er' and 'est' to each root word.

1. rich   _____ _____   4. fat   _____ _____
2. bright   _____ _____   5. hot   _____ _____
3. light   _____ _____   6. big   _____ _____

D. Record the **root word** for each of the following words.

1. tapped   _____   5. baking   _____
2. robber   _____   6. smiled   _____
3. scrubbed _____   7. runs   _____
4. skipping _____   8. taller   _____

Name: _____   Day 5 | Week 13

A. Auditory Test on the Suffixes 's, es, ed, ing, er, est, ly, less, ful'

1. s ed ing	2. er est ed	3. s es est	4. ly less ful	5. s ing ed
6. ed er est	7. ly est ful	8. s less est	9. ing ly ed	10. less ly ful

B. Visual Discrimination Test on the Suffixes 's, es, ed, er, est, ly, less, y'

1. The _____ boy sat by himself and cried. (lone)

2. Playing with matches could be _____. (harm)

3. The _____ man looked sad and very dirty. (home)

4. We like to go _____ in the mountains in Alberta. (hike)

5. Peter's dog is _____ than mine. (big)

6. Mark lives in the _____ house on our street. (large)

7. My mother _____ great peanut butter cookies. (make)

8. Her _____ makes me feel very happy. (smile)

9. Nancy always has the _____ printing. (neat)

10. The bird _____ on the window with its beak. (tap)

Week 14: Adding Suffixes to Root Words

Objective: To teach the rules used to add suffixes to words.

Day 1: On a chart record the following words: sleep, squeak, dusty, stick. Have the students say the words and tell you if the words are things you can see or things you can do. Add the suffix 'y' to each word: sleepy, squeaky, dusty, sticky. Have the students say the words. Discuss what has happened to the meaning of the words. (They tell how something looks, feels, or sounds.) Record these words on the chart: cranky, lumpy, frosty, hairy. Discuss their meanings and have the students use each one in a good sentence.

Activity Worksheet: Page 87 **A.** The students are to record each noun as an adjective by adding the suffix 'y'. **Answer Key: A.** 1. wormy 2. snowy 3. rainy 4. bumpy 5. squeaky 6. rocky 7. thirsty 8. healthy 9. rusty 10. tricky **B.** 1. rocky 2. thirsty 3. healthy 4. wormy 5. snowy 6. rusty 7. rainy 8. squeaky 9. tricky 10. bumpy

Day 2: On a chart record the following words: 1. break 2. wash 3. read 4. love. Discuss each word. What does 'break' mean? (something can fall apart) If something can be broken we add the suffix 'able' to the root word to make the word 'breakable.' The suffix 'able' can be added to wash, read and love. Examples: washable, readable, lovable. Which root word was changed before the suffix 'able' was added? (love) What happened? (The 'e' on love was dropped and then the suffix 'able' was added.) Remind your students of the following rule: When a word ends in a silent 'e', the 'e' is dropped before adding a suffix that begins with a vowel. On the same chart record these words: fall, gold, light, broke. Add the suffix 'en' to each word by following the same rule. (fallen, golden, lighten, broken)

Activity Worksheet: Page 88 **A.** The students are to record the root word for each extended word. **Answer Key: A.** 1. break 2. like 3. soft 4. train 5. dark 6. clean 7. hard 8. love 9. bright 10. wash 11. broke 12. sink **B.** The students are to complete each sentence using a word from Part A. **Answer Key:** 1. breakable 2. likable 3. washable 4. breakable 5. cleanable 6. lovable 7. soften 8. brighten

Day 3: Review the suffixes 'y, en, and able'. On a chart, record the suffixes across the top. Down the chart record the following words: hard, sink, soft, dirt, like, cloud, burn, bright, rock. Rewrite each word adding the suffixes. <u>Possible Answers:</u> harden, hardy, sinkable, softer, dirty, likeable, cloudy, burner, burnable, brighter, rocky

Activity Worksheet: Page 89 The students are to circle the words with the designated suffix in the sentences and then record the root word on the line at the end of it. **Answer Key:** 1. straighten, straight 2. frighten, fright 3. darken, dark 4. Frosty, frost 5. readable, read 6. washable, wash 7. sunny, sun 8. broken, broke 9. wooden, wood 10. breakable, break 11. believable, believe 12. mucky, muck

Day 4: Record the following suffix rules on a chart in two different places. **Rule #1:** If a word ends with a 'y' that has a consonant before it, you change the 'y' to an 'i' and add the suffix 'es.' Have the students practise the rule with the following words: fairy _____, party _____, candy _____, puppy _____, berry _____ **Rule #2:** If a word ends with a 'y' that has a vowel ahead of it, you just add the suffix 's'. Have the students practise the rule with the following words. Words: day (days), toy (toys), rat (rats), key (keys), cob, (cobs)

Activity Worksheet: Page 90 **A.** The students are to make each word plural and to record the number of the rule that they followed. **Answer Key: A.** 1. cherries (1) 2. boys (2) 3. daisies (1) 4. days (2) 5. monkeys (2) 6. toys (2) 7. babies (1) 8. lilies (1) **B.** The students are to circle the plural word in each sentence and to record its root word on the line. **Answer Key B:** 1. daisies, daisy 2. stories, story 3. rays, ray 4. birds, bird 5. strawberries, strawberry 6. flowers, flower 7. cities, city 8. candles, candle

Day 5: Auditory and Visual Discrimination Tests on the Suffixes 'y, en, able, s, es' Page 91
Auditory Test: The students are to circle the suffix that is to be added to the end of each root word. Listen to each word that I say. Circle the suffix that you hear at the end of each word. **Words:** 1. babies 2. lucky 3. broken 4. flies 5. sinkable 6. ponies 7. bumps 8. likeable 9. darken 10. toys **Answer Key:** 1. ies 2. y 3. en 4. ies 5. able 6. ies 7. s 8. able 9. en 10. s

Visual Discrimination Test: The students are to add the suffix 'es, y, en, able, or s' to the word at the end of each sentence and record it on the line to complete it. **Answer Key:** 1. cherries 2. chimneys 3. monkeys 4. parties 5. fairies 6. flies 7. puppies 8. turkeys 9. darken 10. likable

SSR1142 ISBN: 9781771586887 86 © On The Mark Press

Name: _____   Day 1 | Week 14

Sometimes words that are things can be changed into describing words by adding the suffix 'y' to the end of them.

Examples: 1. hair becomes hairy
2. dirt becomes dirty
3. cloud becomes cloudy

A. Change these words into describing words by adding the letter 'y'.

1. worm _____
2. snow _____
3. rain _____
4. bump _____
5. squeak _____
6. rock _____
7. thirst _____
8. health _____
9. rust _____
10. trick _____

B. Use the new words that you made to complete the following sentences.

1. The side of a mountain is very _____ to climb.

2. Playing in the sun makes me very _____.

3. Eating fruit and vegetables makes us very _____.

4. I would not eat the _____ apple in the basket.

5. On _____ days I like to slide down a hill on my toboggan.

6. The wheels on the old wagon were very _____.

7. On _____ days I play games with my sister.

8. The door made a _____ noise when I pushed it open.

9. Unlocking a door without a key is very _____.

10. The road to my uncle's farm was very _____.

Name: _____   Day 2 | Week 14

Don't forget this rule!

When a word ends in a **silent** 'e' drop the 'e' before **adding** a **suffix** that begins with a **vowel**.

Examples: love lovable; broke broken

A. On the line beside each word record its root word.

1. breakable _____   7. harden   _____

2. likable   _____   8. lovable   _____

3. soften   _____   9. brighten   _____

4. trainable _____   10. washable   _____

5. darken   _____   11. broken   _____

6. cleanable _____   12. sinkable   _____

B. Complete each sentence using a word from Part A.

1. If we can break something, we say it is _____.

2. If we like something, we say it is _____.

3. If something can be washed, we say it is _____.

4. If something breaks and falls apart we say it is _____.

5. If something dirty can be cleaned we say it is _____.

6. If someone or something can be loved, we say they are _____.

7. If we make something soft we _____ it.

8. If we cause something to have light, we _____ it.

Name: _____   Day 3 | Week 14

Many **root words** have **suffixes** added at the end.

The suffixes '**y, en** and **able**' are often seen at the ends of words.

Search for the suffixes '**y, en**, and **able**' found in the sentences.

Circle the word that ends with a **suffix** in each sentence and **record** its **root word** on the line at the end of it.

1. The children were told to straighten up their playroom. _____

2. Lisa did not want to frighten Jeff. _____

3. Close the blinds to darken the room for the film. _____

4. Frosty the Snowman led the children through the town. _____

5. Michael's printing was not always readable. _____

6. Most of the clothes that we wear are washable. _____

7. This morning it was sunny and very warm outside. _____

8. The little boy had a broken leg. _____

9. The wooden soldiers were lined up on a shelf. _____

10. Things made of glass are breakable if dropped. _____

11. Fairy tales are not believable stories. _____

12. We tried to drive down the mucky road and got stuck. _____

Name: _____ | Day 4 | Week 14

Don't forget these rules!

1. If a word ends with 'y' that has a **consonant** before it, change the 'y' to an 'i' and then add the suffix '**es**'.

   Example: berry - berr**ies**

2. If a word ends with a 'y' that has a vowel before it, you just add the suffix '**s**'.

   Example: toy - toys

A. Record the word that means more than one on the line and the number of the rule to follow.

Example: berries <u>berry</u> <u>1</u>

1. cherry _____ Rule: ___   5. monkey _____ Rule: ___

2. boy _____ Rule: ___   6. toy _____ Rule: ___

3. daisy _____ Rule: ___   7. baby _____ Rule: ___

4. day _____ Rule: ___   8. lily _____ Rule: ___

B. Circle each word in the sentences that means more than one. Record its **root word** on the line.

1. The field beside our house was full of white daisies. _____

2. I like to read funny stories. _____

3. The rays of the sun were very hot. _____

4. Some birds like to stay in Canada all winter. _____

5. I like to eat strawberries with some ice cream. _____

6. The flowers in the garden began to bloom. _____

7. Many people like to live in cities in Canada. _____

8. We lit seven candles on the birthday cake. _____

Name: _____   Day 5 | Week 14

A. Auditory Discrimination Test on the Suffixes 'y, en, able, s, es'

1.	2.	3.	4.	5.
s ies y	y en s	es y en	ies s able	ies able en
6.	7.	8.	9.	10.
ies able en	ies s en	en able y	able es en	ies s y

B. Visual Discrimination Test on the Suffixes 'y, en, able, s, es'

1. _____ are a bright red fruit. (cherry)

2. _____ take out smoke. (chimney)

3. _____ live in jungles and zoos. (monkey)

4. Birthday _____ are fun to have and to go to. (party)

5. In some tales _____ can do tricks with their wands. (fairy)

6. _____ are black bugs that like to fly around food. (fly)

7. The _____ spilled their dish of milk all over the floor. (puppy)

8. _____ are big birds that are eaten on special days. (turkey)

9. I knew a storm was coming when the sky began to _____. (dark)

10. Our new teacher was pretty and very _____. (like)

Week 15: Adding the Suffixes 'es' to Words Ending With 'ss, x, ch, sh, f, fe'

Objective: To teach the various rules pertaining to adding the **suffix** 'es' to certain words.

Day 1: Teach adding the suffix 'es' to words that end with 'ss' and 'x'. Record the following words on a chart: 1. glass ___ 2. grass ___ 3. pass ___ 4. dress ___ Discuss how you could make each word mean more than one. Can you add the letter 's'? (No) What do you think should be added to words that end with an 's' to make them mean more than one. (You could add 'es'.) Complete the words on the chart. Record this group of words: 1. fox ___ 2. box ___ 3. fix ___ 4. mix ___. Use the same approach used for the words ending with 'ss'. Add 'es' to each word ending with an 'x'.

Activity Worksheet: Page: 93 **A.** The students are to record the plural form of words ending with 'ss' and 'x'. **B.** Students are to underline the plural word in each sentence and then record its root word on the line at the end of it.
Answer Key: A. 1. boxes 2. glasses 3. foxes 4. passes 5. guesses 6. taxes 7. sixes 8. dresses 9. crosses 10. classes **B.** 1. foxes, fox 2. kisses, kiss 3. classes, class 4. glasses, glass 5. boxes, box 6. crosses, cross 7. dresses, dress 8. mixes, mix 9. guesses, guess 10. messes, mess

Day 2: Teach adding the suffix 'es' to words ending with the digraphs 'sh' and 'ch'. On a chart record the following words: bush ___, flash ___, fish ___ ash ___. Tell your students that you are going to make each word plural. At the end of each word record 'es'. What did I do to make each word plural? (added the suffix 'es') Record these words on the chart: match ___, watch ___, church ___, patch ___. Make these words plural by adding the suffix 'es.' What did I do to the end of each word? (added the suffix 'es') Record the words dress ___, glass ___, box ___, fox ___ on the chart. What do we have to do to make these words plural? (add es) Let's make up a rule about adding the suffix 'es' to the ends of words. **Rule:** If a word ends with ss, x, ch, or sh you add the suffix 'es' to the root word to make it mean more than one.

Activity Worksheet: Page 94 **A.** The students are to record each word with the correct suffix. **B.** In each sentence the students are to underline each plural word and then to record its root word on the line provided. **Answer Key: A.** 1. crosses 2. matches 3. sixes 4. dishes 5. dresses 6. churches 7 branches 8. boxes 9. foxes 10. bunches 11. peaches 12. wishes **B.** 1. ranches, ranch, horses, horse 2. patches, patch 3. boxes, box, presents, present 4. bushes, bush 5. classes, class 6. matches, match 7. dishes dish 8. churches church

Day 3: Teach the following rule: In words ending in 'f' or 'fe' you usually change the 'f' or 'fe' to a 'v' before adding the suffix 'es.' On a chart print the rule. Under the rule record the following words: knife, wolf, shelf, leaf. Discuss the rule and have the students tell how to record the words to make them mean more than one.
Words: 1. knife (knives) 2. calf (calves) 3. leaf (leaves) 4. thief (thieves) 5. hoof (hooves)

Activity Worksheet: Page 95 **A.** The students will record the plural form for each word. **B.** The students are to underline the plural word in each sentence and to record its root word on the line at the end of it.
Answer Key: A. 1. lives 2. hooves 3. elves 4. leaves 5. shelves 6. wives 7. halves 8. wolves 9. loaves 10. scarves 11. calves 12. thieves **B.** 1. elves, elf, toys, toy 2. wolves, wolf 3. leaves, leaf 4. calves, calf 5. knives, knife 6. shelves, shelf 7. thieves, thief 8. loaves, loaf 9. dwarves, drawf 10. scarves, scarf

Day 4: Review adding the suffix 'es' to words ending in 'ss, x, sh, f, and fe. On a chart record the following words down one side: 1. cross 2. church 3. box 4. bush 5. leaf 6. life . Have the students record each word's plural form and explain what they had to do to each word.

Activity Worksheet: Page 96: **A.** The students will record each word in its plural form. **B.** The students will record the plural form of the root word in the brackets in each sentence. **Answer Key: A.** 1. kisses 2. waxes 3. patches 4. foxes 5. halves 6. bushes 7. knives 8. passes 9. boxes **B.** 1. leaves 2. dishes 3. matches 4. shelves 5. brushes 6. boxes 7. ourselves 8. hooves 9. elves 10. stores

Day 5: Auditory and Visual Discrimination Test on Adding the Suffixes 'es' to Words Ending in 'ss, x, sh, f, and fe' Page: 97
A. Auditory Test: The students are to listen to the word spoken by the teacher and to circle the suffix that would be at its end. **Words:** 1. knives 2. crosses 3. leaves 4. cherries 5. books 6. boxes 7. bushes 8. matches **Answer Key:** 1. ves 2. es 3. ves 4. ies 5. s 6. es 7. es 8. es

B. Visual Discriination Test: The students are to underline the plural word in each sentence and to record its root word on the line. **Answer Key:** 1. knives, knife 2. wishes, wish 3. elves, elf 4. ranches, ranch 5. brushes, brush 6. foxes, fox, farms, farm 7. dresses, dress 8. waxes, wax, candles, candle 9. wolves, wolf 10. calves, calf

Name: _____   Day 1 | Week 15

What a load! Rules! Rules! More Rules!

When a word ends with an 'x' or 'ss' the suffix 'es' is added to make it mean more than one.

Examples: box   box**es**   dress   dress**es**

A. Make the following words mean more than one.

1. box   _____
2. glass _____
3. fox   _____
4. pass   _____
5. guess _____

6. tax   _____
7. six   _____
8. dress _____
9. cross _____
10. class _____

B. **Underline** each word that means more than one in each sentence and record its **root word** on the line.

1. The forest was full of very hungry foxes. _____

2. The little girl blew kisses to her father at the window. _____

3. How many classes are at your school. _____

4. My glasses fell on the floor and broke. _____

5. The boxes were piled high in the old attic. _____

6. Crosses are seen at the top of many churches. _____

7. Which of these dresses do you like the best? _____

8. My mother uses cake mixes when she bakes. _____

9. Your guesses are always correct. _____

10. Who made all the messes on the floor. _____

Name: _____   Day 2 | Week 15

Remember this rule!

If a word ends in '**ss**, **x**, **sh**, or **ch** you usually add the suffix '**es**' to the end of it to make it mean more than one.

Examples: guess**es**   box**es**   bush**es**   watch**es**

A. Make each of the words below mean more than one.

1. cross _____   5. dress _____   9. fox _____

2. match _____   6. church _____   10. bunch _____

3. six _____   7. branch _____   11. peach _____

4. dish _____   8. box _____   12. wish _____

B. Underline each word that means more than one in each sentence and record its root word on the line.

1. People like to visit ranches in Alberta to ride on horses. _____

2. The poor man had patches on his pants and coat. _____

3. The boxes under the tree were filled with presents. _____

4. The kitten was hiding behind some bushes. _____

5. Three classes went on a bus trip to the zoo. _____

6. The firefighter told the class not to play with matches. _____

7. Please set the dishes on the table for supper. _____

8. There are six churches in our small town. _____

Name: _____   Day 3 | Week 15

"What a load! Rules! Rules! More Rules"

Here is another rule to remember!

If a word ends with an 'f' or 'fe' you often have to change the 'f' or 'fe' to a 'v' before you add the suffix 'es.'

Examples: wife - wives   leaf - leaves

A. Make the following words mean more than one.

1. life _____
2. hoof _____
3. elf _____
4. leaf _____
5. shelf _____
6. wife _____
7. half _____
8. wolf _____
9. loaf _____
10. scarf _____
11. calf _____
12. thief _____

B. Underline the word in each sentence that means more than one. **Record** its **root word** on the line at the end of the sentence.

1. The elves, at the North Pole, were busy making toys. _____

2. I heard the wolves howling late last night. _____

3. By the end of November there will be no leaves on the tree. _____

4. At the barn on the farm we saw some calves that had just been born. _____

5. Some people use sharp knives for carving wood. _____

6. The boy kept all his toy cars on shelves in his bedroom. _____

7. Some thieves stole money from a bank. _____

8. The baker made seven loaves of white bread. _____

9. The seven dwarves saved Snow White from the bad witch. _____

10. My grandmother loves to knit scarves with colourful wool. _____

Name: _____   Day 4 | Week 15

Don't forget these rules!

What a load! Rules! Rules! More Rules!

1. If a word ends with 'ss, x, ch or sh' you add 'es' to make it mean more than one or plural.

   Examples: grasses, boxes, bunches, brushes

2. If a word ends with 'f' or 'fe' you often change the 'f' or 'fe' to the letter 'v' before adding the suffix 'es.'

   Examples: knives, lives, thieves

A. Record the **plural** for each of the following words.

   1. kiss _____   4. fox _____   7. knife _____

   2. wax _____   5. half _____   8. pass _____

   3. patch _____   6. bush _____   9. box _____

B. Record the **plural** for each root word in the brackets at the end of each sentence on the line in the sentence.

   1. In the fall, _____ change their colour and then fall off. (leaf)

   2. Tony helped his mother by drying the _____. (dish)

   3. Children should not play with _____. (match)

   4. My father painted the _____ in the kitchen for my mother. (shelf)

   5. We used wire _____ to scrape off the old paint. (brush)

   6. How many _____ of cookies do you have to sell. (box)

   7. We cleaned up the barn all by _____. (ourself)

   8. Horseshoes are put on the _____ of horses. (hoof)

   9. The _____ made shoes for the old shoemaker late at night. (elf)

   10. Nancy loves to visit _____ that have lots of toys. (store)

Name: _____   Day 5 | Week 15

A. Auditory Test on Suffixes 'ves, es, ies, s

1. s ves es	2. es s ies	3. ies ves es	4. ves s ies
5. es ies s	6. ies es ves	7. s es ies	8. es e ies

B. Visual Discrimination Test on the Suffixes 'ves, es, ies, s'

1. My mother took her knives to a store to have them sharpened. _____

2. At the wishing well I made three wishes. _____

3. Some elves like to trick people. _____

4. Men work on ranches to look after cattle. _____

5. These brushes are used for painting a picture. _____

6. Foxes like to live in a forest near farms. _____

7. I made three new dresses for my Barbie doll. _____

8. Some waxes are used to make candles. _____

9. Wolves are often heard howling late at night. _____

10. Our calves won first prize at the fall fair. _____

Week 16: Syllabication

Objective: To develop the recognition of syllables in words containing suffixes

Day 1: On a chart record the two syllable words that have suffixes. **Words:** cloudy, careful, faster, cleanest, golden, trying, nicely. Have the students underline the root word and circle the suffix in each word. Then have them clap each word and record the number of syllables heard at the end of each one. Explain to your students a root word becomes a two syllable word when it has a suffix added to the end of it.

Activity Worksheet: Page 99 **A.** The students are to underline the root word and to circle the suffix in each word. **B.** The students are to use the words in the Word Box to complete each sentence. **Answer Key: A.** 1. home less 2. big gest 3. love ly 4. play ful 5. talk ing 6. clean ing 7. loud est 8. dark ness 9. bright en 10. paint ed 11. slow ly 12. hunt er **B.** playful 2. lovely 3. painted 4. talking 5. loudest 6. cleaning 7. homeless 8. slowly 9. loudest 10. darkness 11. hunter 12. brighten

Day 2: Review the suffixes that can be added to one syllable words. On a chart record the following syllables at the top of it. **Suffixes:** ing, s, es, ed, ves, y, en, able, less, ness, er, ly, ful. In a column down the chart record the following root words: 1. like 2. neat 3. beg 4. love 5. catch 6. store 7. cross 8. box Have the students add as many different suffixes to each root word and note the changes. **Answers:** 1.likes, liked, liking, likable 2. neatness, neater, neatly 3. begs, begged, begging, begger 4. loves, loved, loving, lovable, lovely 5. catches, catching, catcher 6. stores, stored, storing, story 7. crosses, crossed, crossing 8. box, boxes, boxing, boxed, boxer

Activity Worksheet: Page 100 The students will add the correct suffixes to each root word. **Answer Key:** 1. helpless, helper, helpful, helps, helped, helping 2. neatly, neatness, neater 3. stores, stored, storing, story, stories 4. loves, loved, loving, lovable, lovely 5. kinds, kinder, kindly, kindness 6. dances, danced, dancing, dancer 7. likes, liked, liking, likable, likely 8. washes, washed, washing washable, washer

Day 3: Have the students practise dividing words into syllables using a stroke mark (/). Record the following words on a chart. **Words:** homeless, painted, neatly, parties, careful, louder, darkness, brighten, cloudy, walking, helps, begged, helping.

Activity Worksheet: Page 101 **A.** The students will circle the syllable that could be added to each word. **Answer Key:** 1. ing 2. s 3. less 4. es 5. ves 6. es 7. y 8. es 9. er 10. es **B.** The students will complete each sentence with the correct word. **Answer Key:** 1. blooming 2. brushes 3. ranches 4. guessed 5. brighten 6. watches 7. peaches 8. calves

Day 4: Review root words with suffixes. Record the following words on a chart. **Words:** painted, brighten, slowly, careless, louder, eating, lighten, spoonful, patches, rainy, sinkable. Have the students underline the root words and circle the suffixes.

Activity Worksheet: Page 102 **A.** The students are to record the number of syllables heard in each word. Answer Key: 1. (2) 2. (2) 3. (2) 4. (1) 5. (1) 6. (1) 7. (2) 8. (2) 9. (1) 10. (2) 11. (2) 12. (1) 13. (2) 14. (1) 15. (2) **B.** The students are to record the correct word in each sentence. **Answer Key:** 1. turkeys 2. glasses 3. quickly 4. thirsty 5. sickness 6. careless 7. training 8. eating 9. cloudy 10. gladly 11. careful 12. slowly

Day 5: Auditory and Visual Discrimination Test on Syllabication Page 103

A. Auditory Test: The students will circle the suffix that they hear at the end of each word said by the teacher. **Words:** 1. walked 2. painful 3. knives 4. likable 5. weakness 6. lucky 7. daisies 8. hopeless 9. quickly **Answer Key:** 1. ed 2. ful 3. ves 4. able 5. ness 6. y 7. ies 8. less 9. ly

B. Visual Discrimination Test: The students will add a suffix to each word to complete the sentence. **Answer Key:** 1. en 2. ies 3. ful 4. ves 5. ly 6. ful 7. ness 8. y 9. able 10. es, ves

Name: _____   Day 1 | Week 16

Here's another rule to remember!

When a root word has a suffix added to its ending it may become a two syllable word.

Examples: highest careless rainy thankful wooden

A. In the word box, **circle** the root word and **underline** the suffix in each word.

Word Box

1. homeless
2. biggest
3. lovely
4. playful
5. talking
6. cleaning
7. loudest
8. darkness
9. brighten
10. painted
11. slowly
12. hunter

B. Complete eah sentence with a word from the Word Box.

1. The new puppy was very cute and _____.
2. The girl who sang O Canada had a _____ voice.
3. We _____ pictures of our trip to the zoo at school.
4. I like _____ to my friends on my cell phone.
5. My big brother can yell the _____ in our family.
6. The lady next door was busy _____ her windows.
7. The big forest fire in Alberta made many people _____.
8. The cars moved very _____ on the busy highway.
9. The drums in the band made the _____ boom.
10. The _____ of the room made me feel afraid.
11. The _____ used a bow and arrow to kill deer.
12. The sun will _____ our world when it shines.

Name: _____ Day 2 | Week 16

Remember: A **syllable** is a group of letters or a letter added to the **end** of a root word.

A suffix is a syllable.

Examples: church**es** sick**ness** part**ies** loud**ly** snow**y** jump**ed** walk**ing** pick**s**

A. Add as many suffixes to each of the following root words as you can.

Suffixes
s   es   ed   ing   ves   y   en   able   less   ness   er   ly   ful   ies

Example: dress - dress**es**, dress**ed**, dress**ing**, dress**er**

1. help: _____

2. neat: _____

3. store: _____

4. love: _____

5. kind: _____

6. dance: _____

7. like: _____

8. wash: _____

Name: _____   Day 3 | Week 16

A root word + a suffix = 2 syllables

A **root word** with a **suffix** often contains **two** syllables.

Examples: useful   slowly   rainy   careless

A. Which suffix can you add to each word? Circle the correct one.

1. train	ing	ly	en	6. match	s	es	ies
2. pain	ly	er	s	7. cloud	y	ful	ly
3. home	en	er	less	8. class	s	ies	es
4. dish	ies	s	es	9. neat	sh	fe	er
5. elf	es	ies	ves	10. bush	er	es	en

B. Complete each sentence with the correct word.

| ranches | calves | watches | guessed | brushes |
| peaches | brighten | useless | cheerful | blooming |

1. Look at all the tulips _____ in the garden this spring.

2. Jill _____ her dog's fur every Saturday morning.

3. Cattle and horses are kept on _____ in the province of Alberta.

4. John _____ the right answer to the teacher's question.

5. Nathan gave his teacher a rose to _____ her day.

6. _____ are used to tell us the time.

7. I picked one of the yellow _____ to eat from the bowl.

8. The young _____ followed the cows into the field.

Name: _____   Day 4 | Week 16

Remember: Syllables are word parts.

Examples: paint + ed = painted
   slow + ly = slowly
   spoon + ful = spoonful

Syllables are word parts.

A. Record the **number** of syllables heard in each word.

1. chimneys ____   6. glad ____   11. biggest ____
2. sickness ____   7. flowers ____   12. half ____
3. rolling ____   8. puppy ____   13. useful ____
4. plays ____   9. kiss ____   14. card ____
5. rain ____   10. homeless ____   15. slowly ____

B. Record the **word** in the Word Box that matches each **meaning**.

| eating | training | careless | slowly | sickness | thirsty |
| glasses | turkeys | cloudy | gladly | careful | quickly |

1. kind of birds _____   7. teaching _____

2. worn on the face _____   8. munching _____

3. a way to move fast _____   9. not clear _____

4. need a drink _____   10. happy _____

5. illness _____   11. move with care _____

6. not caring _____   12. not fast _____

Name: _____ Day 5 | Week 16

A. Auditory Test on the Suffixes 's, es, ing, ed, ful, ly, en, y, ness, les, er, able, ves'

1. ing ed s	2. ful les y	3. ness less ves
4. en able y	5. ly ness ed	6. able en y
7. ies es s	8. er less ing	9. ves es ly

B. Visual Descrimination Test on the Suffixes:

Add a suffix to each word to complete each sentence.

s, es, ing, ed, ful, ly, en, y, ness, ies, er, able, less, ves

1. The sun will bright_____ the day.

2. Birthday part_____ are fun to have.

3. We picked a basket_____ of cherries from the tree.

4. The lea_____ on the trees change their colours in the fall.

5. The lady looked love ____ in her new dress.

6. Breaking a leg would be pain _____.

7. The children's kind_____ made the old lady happy

8. It is not safe to drive on a very snow_____ day.

9. Things made of glass are break_____.

10. Fox_____ and wol_____ are forest animals.

SSR1142 ISBN: 9781771586887   103   © On The Mark Press

Week 17: Regular Double Vowels 'ea, ee, ai, oa, ie, ay, ow'

Objective: To make students aware of the regular double vowels and their sounds.

Day 1: On a chart, record the following words: beads, feet, fair, boat, tie, leaf, hay. Have the students read each word aloud. Discuss the words: How many vowels do you see in each word? (two) How many vowels do you hear in each one? (first vowel) Is it making the long or short vowel sound? (long vowel sound) Explain this rule: If a one part word or syllable has two vowels, the first vowel usually makes the long sound and the second is silent.

Picture Key: Row 1: beach, feet, chair, goat Row 2: pie, train, hay, snow

Activity Worksheet: Page 105 **A.** The students are to complete the words under each picture with a regular double vowel sound. **Answer Key: A.** Row 1: beach, feet, chair, goat Row 2: pie, train, hay, snow **B.** Students are to use the words they completed in the sentences. **Answer Key:** 1. goat 2. snow 3. feet 4. train 5. chair 6. hay 7. pie 8. beach

Day 2: Review the regular double vowels found in words using these clues. Have the students record the words on a chart. **Clues:** 1. It is a group of players that play a sport. (team) 2. They are found on the sides of your face. (cheeks) 3. It is a path you follow through the mountains. (trail) 4. It is a little brown creature that can hop. (toad) 5. It is worn around the collar of a shirt. (tie) 6. Dishes are carried on me. (tray) 7. I sit on top of a present. (bow) Have the students print each word on a chart and then circle the long vowel sound.

Picture Key: Row 1: coat, sheet, rain, wheat Row 2: tie, tray, snow, beans Row 3: seeds, fairy, boat, pie Row 4: hay, blow, meat, street Row 5: jail, goat, spray, hair

Activity Worksheet: Page 106 **A.** The students will complete each word with the correct vowel combination. **Answer Key:** Row 1: coat, sheet, rain, wheat, Row 2: tie, tray, snow, beans Row 3: seeds, fairy, boat, pie Row 4: hay, blow, meat, street Row 5: jail, goat, spray, hair

Day 3: On a chart record the following double vowels at the top: ea, ee, ai, oa, ie, ay, ou. Below the double vowels record the following incomplete words: 1. fl___t 2. p___n 3. p___r 4. b___t 5. t___l 6. h___l 7. b___ 8. t___d 9. s___l 10. s___d. Have the students use the double vowels to make words and tell what they say. **Possible Words:** float, fleet, pain, pair, pear, beat, beet, boat, bait, tail, hail, heel, bee, toad, tied, sail, seal, seed

Activity Worksheet: Page 107 **A.** The students are to circle words in each sentence that contain a regular double vowel. The circled words are to be listed on the lines under the sentence. **Answer Key:** <u>Circled Words</u> - 1. crow, seed, feeder 2. hay, oats, eat 3. green, paint 4. toad, snail 5. trail, day 6. oak, tree, leaves 7. team, play 8. please, tie **B:** <u>Alphabetical Order</u>: crow, day, eat, feeder, green, hay, leaves, oak, oats, paint, play, please, seed, snail, team, tie, toad, trail

Day 4: Review the sounds of regular double vowels such as 'ea, ee, ai, oa, ie, ay, ow, On a chart record the double vowels. Under the sounds record the following incomplete words: 1. p___l 2. c___t 3. s___l 4. sn___ 5. t___st 6. p___ 7. pl___ 8. tr___n 9. sw___t 10. h___r 11. fl___t 12. s___t. Have the students record a double vowel sound in each one and say the words. There may be more than one answer for each word.

Activity Worksheet: Page 108 **A.** The students are to read each clue and record the word on the line that answers it. **Answer Key: A.** 1. leaf 2. boat 3. deer 4. train 5. toast 6. pie 7. crow 8. snail 9. May 10. wheels **B.** 1. ow 2. ee, ai, oa 3. ea 4. ea, ai 5. ie 6. ay 7. oa, ee 8. ay, ee 9. ee 10. ay, ow 11. ai 12. ee, ay (Answers may vary)

Day 5: Auditory and Visual Discrimination Test on Regular Double Vowels 'ea, ee, ai, oa, ie, ay, ow'
Page: 109 **Auditory Test:** The students will circle the double vowel sound that they hear in each word spoken by the teacher. **Words:** 1. tie 2. float 3. bee 4. paint 5. team 6. bow 7. day 8. rain
Answer Key: 1. ie 2. oa 3. ee 4. ai 5. ea 6. ow 7. ay 8. ai
Visual Discrimination Test: The students will circle the double vowel that will complete the unfinished word in each sentence and record it on the line. **Answer Key:** 1. ow 2. ie 3. ea 4. ea 5. ea 6. ay 7. ie 8. oa 9. ee 10. ai

Name: _____ Day 1 | Week 17

Remember! In a one syllable word, that has two vowels together, the **first vowel** does all the talking and makes the **long** vowel sound. The **second vowel** is **silent**.

Examples: coat   rain   sea   free

A. Record the word for each picture on the line in each box.

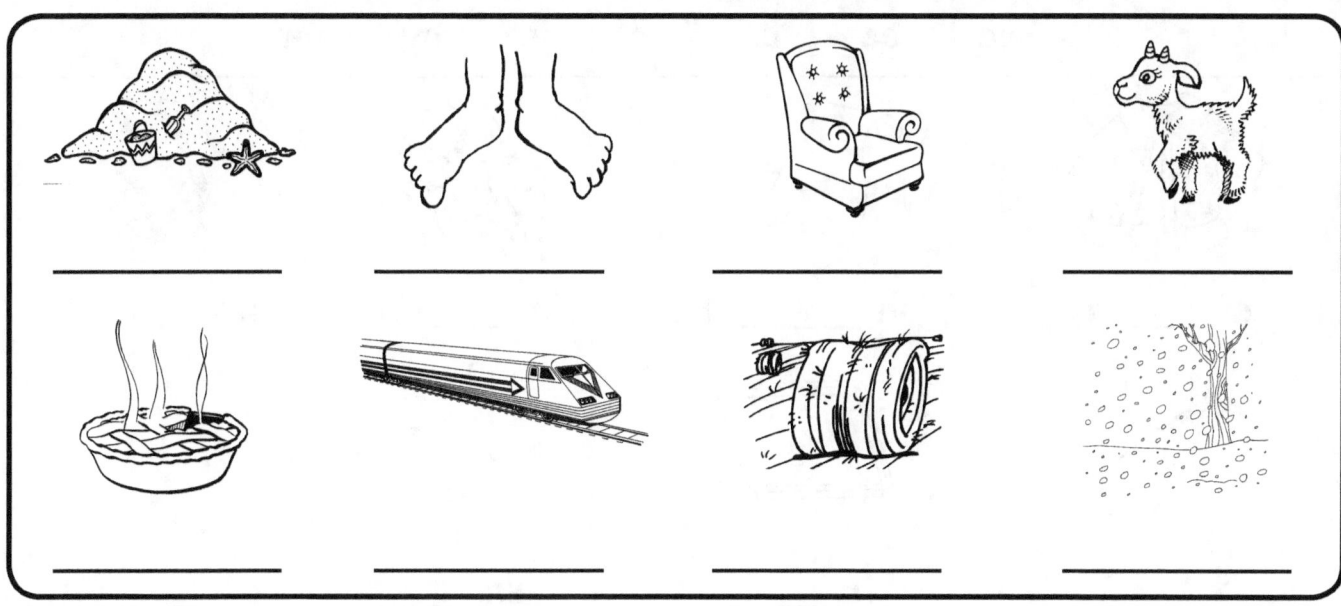

B. Complete the sentences with the picture words.

1. The smallest _____ would not cross the Troll's bridge.

2. It is fun to play games in the _____ during the winter.

3. What kind of shoes do you have on your _____.

4. We travelled to Toronto on a very fast _____.

5. My father falls asleep in his big _____ every night.

6. Many farm animals enjoy munching on _____.

7. Everyone in my family loves my grandmother's pumpkin _____.

8. I love to visit a _____ in Nova Scotia to play in the sand.

Name: _____   Day 2 | Week 17

Remember! A word that has **one** syllable with two vowels together, the **first** vowel is **heard** and the **second** vowel is **silent**.

Examples: eat pain day crow lie goat bee

A. Complete each word with the correct regular double vowel.

oa   ee   ai   ea   ie   ay   ow

c ___ t   sh ___ t   r ___ n   wh ___ t

t ___   tr ___   sn ___   b ___ ns

s ___ ds   f ___ ry   b ___ t   p ___

h ___   bl ___   m ___ t   str ___ t

j ___ l   g ___ t   spr ___   h ___ r

106

Name: _____   Day 3 | Week 17

Remember !

Double vowel words are used in many sentences.

Example: The <u>train</u> ran on <u>steel</u> tracks.

A. Read each sentence carefully. **Circle** the words that contain **regular double vowels**.

1. The black crow ate all the bird seed in the feeder.
2. The farmer planted hay and oats for his horses to eat.
3. Bill used green paint on the new fence.
4. Harry saw a toad and a snail sitting on a rock.
5. We rode our horses on the trail all day.
6. On an oak tree there are many leaves.
7. My team will play hockey at the rink.
8. Please tie a rope around the box.

B. Record the words that you circled in alphabetical order on the lines.

_____   _____   _____

_____   _____   _____

_____   _____   _____

_____   _____   _____

_____   _____   _____

_____   _____   _____

Name: _____ Day 4 | Week 17

Remember this rule!

In a one syllable word that has two vowels together, the first vowel does all the talking and makes the second vowel be quiet.

A. Read each clue. Record the word on the line that matches it.

1. It grows on a tree. _____

2. You can travel on water in it. _____

3. It is a forest animal that is hunted in the fall. _____

4. It travels very fast on tracks carrying things and people. _____

5. You eat this for breakfast with your favourite jam. _____

6. Apples and cherries are often baked inside one. _____

7. It is a large black bird that caws loudly. _____

8. It lives in a shell and moves very slowly. _____

9. It is the name of a month in the spring. _____

10. A car has four of these that go round and round. _____

B. Complete each word with a double vowel: ea, ee, ai, oa, ie, ay, ow

1. sn _____   5. p _____   9. wh _____ l

2. f _____ l   6. st _____   10. pl _____

3. s _____ t   7. fl _____ t   11. t _____ l

4. s _____ l   8. tr _____   12. tr _____

Name: _____   Day 5 | Week 17

Auditory Test and Visual Discrimination Test on the Regular Double Vowels 'ea, ee, ai, oa, ie, ay, ow'

A. Auditory Test:

1. ee ie ea	2. ow oa ee	3. ow ie ee	4. oa ea ai
5. ea oa ay	6. oa ow ea	7. ai ay oa	8. ay ai oa

B. Visual Discrimination Test:

1. A rooster likes to cr ____ early in the day. (ie, ow, oa)

2. Please t ____ up the laces on your shoes before you trip. (ai, oa, ie)

3. The children sat quietly in their s ____ ts. (ea, oa, ie)

4. My sister gave me a box of p____ nuts for a snack. (oa, ay, ea)

5. The s____l grabbed the fish and quickly ate it. (ie, ea, ow)

6. Put the dishes of food on the tr ____. (ow, ee, ay)

7. My mother fr ____ d the fish in a big pan. (ee, ea, ie)

8. The g ____ t stood at the top of the big pile of hay. (oo, ow, oa)

9. Some candies are very sw ____ t . (ee, ai, ay)

10. The little puppy wagged its t ____ l happily. (oa, ai, ea)

Week 18: Vowel Digraphs 'oo, ea, au, ae, ei'

Objective: To make students aware that vowel digraphs may make two sounds. They may have a long sound and a short sound.

Day 1: On a chart record these two groups of words. **Group 1:** pool, tooth, soon, goose Which vowel digraph do you see and hear in each word? (long vowel 'o' digraph) Record **Group 2** list of words on the chart: look, good, shook, cook. Does the vowel digraph 'oo' make the same sound in these words? (No) The vowel digraph 'oo' has a long sound as in moon and a short sound as in 'hook'. Record these words on the chart: cheat, meat, wheat, beat. Have the students say each word. Discuss the sound that 'ea' makes. (long vowel e) Record these words on the chart: head, bread, lead, weather. What sound does 'ea' make in these words? (short 'e' vowel sound) The vowel digraph 'ea' has a long and a short vowel sound. In the word 'meat' it has a long vowel 'e' sound. In 'head' it has the short vowel 'e' sound.

Picture Key: Row 1: book, feather, eagle, hook, bread Row 2: roof, peach, head, moon, balloon

Activity Worksheet: Page 111 **A.** The students are to record the correct vowel digraph heard in each picture. **Answer Key:** Row 1: short oo, short ea, long ea, short oo, short ea Row 2: long oo, long ea, short ea, long oo, long oo **B.** The students are to complete each sentence with the correct word in the Word Box. **Answer Key:** 1. shook 2. peas 3. leather 4. school 5. weak 6. goose 7. heavy 8. stool 9. good 10. ready

Day 2: On a chart record the following group of words: saw, jaw, crawl, draw, paw. Have the students say the words. Discuss the sound made by the letters 'aw.' Have them notice how their jaws drop when they say each word. On the same chart record the following words: auto, autumn, haul, because, dinosaur. Have the students say each word. Do you hear a sound that is the same as in the first group of words. (Yes) What is the sound? (aw) Which two letters are making the sound in these words? (au) The vowel sounds 'aw' and 'au' make the same sound in words. They are called *irregular double vowels*.

Activity Worksheet: Page 112 **A.** The students will circle all the words in the sentences that have the vowel digraphs 'aw' and 'au.' **Answer Key: A.** 1. autumn 2. yawn 3. dinosaur 4. sauce 5. claws 6. haul 7. thaw 8. hawk, caught, claws 9. daughter, draw 10. Paul's paw **B.** The students will classify the 'au' and 'aw' words.

Answer Key: 'au' Words: autumn, dinosaur, sauce, haul, daughter caught, Paul's 'aw' Words: yawn, claws, paw, thaw, hawk, draw,

Day 3: On a chart record the following words: eight, sleigh, weigh, freight. Underline the 'ei' sound in each word. Explain to the children that the vowel digraph 'ei' makes the same sound as the 'long a'. Have the students say each word.

Activity Worksheet: Page 113 **A.** The students are to record the vowel digraphs 'ai, ei, and ay' to complete each word. **B.** The students are to record words with 'ei' in the correct sentences. **Answer Key: A.** 1. ai 2. ay 3. ei 4. ei 5. ay 6. ai or ei 7. ei 8. ay 9. ei 10. ai 11. ei 12. ai **B.** 1. freighter 2. sleigh 3. weigh 4. veins 5. reindeer 6. reins 7. neighbours 8. neighs 9. eight 10. freight

Day 4: Review the vowel digraphs 'ea, oo, ee, au, ow.' Remind your students that some of the digraphs make two sounds such as 'ea, oo, and ee.' On a chart record these incomplete words and have the students complete them with the vowel digraphs 'ea, oo, ee, au, aw.' **Words:** 1. feather 2. goose 3. peas 4. good 5. year 6. claws 7. sauce 8. reins 9. head 10. boom

Activity Worksheet: Page 114 **A.** The students are to record the number of the digraph rule on the line. **B.** The sentences are to be completed with the correct word. **Answer Key: A.** 1. (3) 2. (2) 3. (1) 4. (2) 5. (1) 6. (4) 7. (3) 8. (2) 9. (4) 10. (2) **B.** 1. August 2. auto 3. eighty 4. jaw 5. eagle 6. crawl 7. yawn 8. veins 9. sauce 10. sleigh

Day 5: Auditory and Visual Discrimination Test on 'oo, ea, au, aw, ei' Page 115

Auditory Test: The students will circle the digraph in each box heard in the word spoken by the teacher. **Words:** 1. tooth 2. meat 3. hook 4. because 5. weigh 6. ready 7. caw 8. fair **Answer Key:** 1. oo 2. ea 3. oo 4. au 5. ei 6. ea 7. aw 8. ai

Visual Discrimination Test: The students will record the correct word in each sentence.
Answer Key: 1. weak 2. eagle, claws 3. goose, eight 4. reins 5. brook, clear 6. lawn, green, rain 7. sauce, cream 8. caught 9. leather

© On The Mark Press

Name: _____ Day 1 | Week 18

The vowel digraph 'oo' has **two** sounds. Sometimes it says 'oo' as in '**book**' or '**oo**' as in '**tools**.'

The vowel digraph '**ea**' has two sounds too. In some words it has the long '**ea**' sound as in '**beat**' and in other words it may have the short '**e**' sound as in '**head**.'

A. Which vowel digraph do you hear in each picture. Is it the long 'ea', short 'ea', long 'oo' or the short 'oo' sound? **Record** the digraph that you hear on the line in each box.

B. **Complete** each sentence with the correct word from the Word Box.

stool	goose	school	leather	ready
good	shook	peas	weak	heavy

1. The dog _____ himself when it came out of the lake.

2. _____ and carrots are often mixed together.

3. A saddle for a horse is made out of _____.

4. Soon the children will be going back to _____.

5. The sick child was too _____ to get out of bed.

6. The young _____ had trouble flying with the flock.

7. The rock was too _____ to pick up.

8. I had to stand on a _____ to reach the book on the shelf.

9. Most children try to be _____ at school.

10. The teams were _____ to play a game of hockey.

Name: _____   Day 2 | Week 18

Sometimes vowel digraphs make the same sound in words.

The vowel digraphs '**au**' and '**aw**' both make the same sound.

Examples: **au:** sauce, autumn, auto

aw: lawn, paw, crawl

The vowel digraphs au and aw make the same sounds.

A. The sounds '**aw**' and '**au**' are called **irregular double vowels**. Circle the words in the sentences that have an irregular double vowel.

 1. In the autumn, the leaves fall off the trees.

 2. Please cover your mouth when you yawn.

 3. A dinosaur was a large animal that lived many years ago.

 4. I like to put chocolate sauce on my ice cream.

 5. The tiger had long sharp claws on his feet.

 6. The truck will haul all the dirt away.

 7. In the spring, the snow and ice begin to thaw.

 8. The hawk caught the rabbit with its very sharp claws.

 9. My daughter likes to draw pictures.

 10. Paul's dog cut its paw on some glass.

B. Make a list of the '**au**' and '**aw**' words that you found in the sentences.

'**au**' Words	'**aw**' words
_____	_____
_____	_____
_____	_____
_____	_____
_____	_____
_____	_____

Name: _____   Day 3 | Week 18

The long vowel 'a' sound is also made by the two letters 'ei' in some words.

Examples: eight   eighty   eighteen

There are also other vowel groups that make the long 'a' sound in words. They are 'ai' and 'ay.'

Examples: fair   chair   play   may

A. Which vowel sound have you heard and have seen in each word below. Is it 'ei, ai or ay.' Record the correct sound in each word.

1. h ____ r
2. pl ____ er
3. v ____ ns
4. w ____ ghs
5. cr ____ on
6. r ____ n
7. sl ____ gh
8. pr ____
9. r ____ ndeer
10. sn ____ l
11. n ____ gh
12. tr ____ l

B. Use the following 'ei' words in the sentences

| weigh | neighs | sleigh | freight | neighbour |
| freighter | veins | reindeer | reins | eight |

1. A _____ is a large ship that carries many things.
2. It is fun to ride in a _____ pulled by a horse.
3. The doctor will _____ you during your checkup.
4. The _____ in your body carry blood to every part.
5. Santa's _____ travelled high in the sky over many houses.
6. I had to pull hard on the _____ to get my horse to stop.
7. Our _____ helped my dad build a fence.
8. A horse is saying hello when it _____.
9. My brother will soon be _____ years old.
10. The _____ train zoomed along the tracks heading towards Winnipeg.

Name: _____ Day 4 | Week 18

Remember these rules!

1. The vowel digraph 'ea' has two sounds. It may have a long 'e' or a short 'e' sound.
2. The vowel digraph 'oo' has two sounds. It may say 'oo' as in 'book' or 'oo' as in 'tools.'
3. The vowel digraph 'ei' makes the long vowel 'a' sound in words.
4. The vowel digraphs 'au' and 'aw' make the same sound.

A. Which rule does each of the following words follow? Record its rule number on the line.

1. reins   Rule _____
2. brook   Rule _____
3. bread   Rule _____
4. balloon   Rule _____
5. beach   Rule _____
6. lawn   Rule _____
7. weight   Rule _____
8. goose   Rule _____
9. sauce   Rule _____
10. roof   Rule _____

B. Use the following words to match each of the clues.

| eagle | jaw | eighty | auto | crawl |
| August | yawn | veins | sauce | sleigh |

1. It is the name of a summer month. _____
2. It is another name for car. _____
3. It follows the number seventy-nine. _____
4. It is the lower part of your face. _____
5. It likes to live in high places. _____
6. It is a way to move close to the floor. _____
7. It is done when someone is very tired. _____
8. They are like rivers running through our bodies. _____
9. It is something sweet to put on ice cream. _____
10. It is used for winter travelling on snow. _____

Name: _____ Day 5 | Week 18

Auditory and Visual Discrimination Test on th Digraphs 'oo,ea,au,aw,ei'

A. Auditory Test:

1. ei oo ea	2. ea oo aw	3. oa ea oo	4. oo ea au
5. oo ee ei	6. ee ea ei	7. oo aw ea	8. au oa ai

B. Visual Discrimination Test:

leather	goose	lawn	reins	brook
sauce	caught	eight	eagle	green
claws	clear	rain	weak	cream

1. The sick old man was too _____ to walk very far.

2. The _____ grabbed the rabbit with its _____.

3. The _____ honked loudly at her _____ babies.

4. Pull on the _____ tightly and the horse will stop.

5. In the spring, the _____ is filled with cold, _____ water.

6. The grass on the _____ was very _____ after the _____.

7. I love to have chocolate _____ on my ice _____.

8. The little grey mouse was _____ in the trap.

9. Some shoes are made of _____.

Week 19: Diphthongs oi, oy, ou, ow, ew

Objective: To teach the recognition of the sounds made by the diphthongs 'oi, oy, ou, ow, ew'

Day 1: On a chart record the following groups of words: **Group 1** - boy, toy, joy; **Group 2** - boil, coin, point. Discuss the words in Group 1 with your students. Have the students say each word. Have them tell how each word is the same. (end with the same letters that make the same sound) Where is this sound found in the words? (at the end) What letters make the sound? (oy) Discuss Group 2 with your students. Have your students tell how these words are the same. (They have the same sound in the middle of the words.) Compare the location of 'oy' and 'oi' in a word. ('oy' is found at the end of a word while 'oi' is found inside a word and sometimes at the beginning of one.)

Activity Worksheet: Page 117 **A.** The students are to complete each word with the correct diphthong 'oi' or 'oy'. **B.** The students will use the words in the Word Box in the correct sentence. **Answer Key: A.** 1. oi 2. oy 3. oy 4. oi 5. oi 6. oi 7. oy 8. oy 9. oi **B.** 1. coins 2. destroy 3. joint 4. decoy 5. point 6. joy 7. boy 8. voice 9. spoil 10. annoy

Day 2: On a chart record the following groups of words. **Group 1:** cloud, found, house, ouch **Group 2:** bow, clown, how, down Discuss the words in Group 1. Have the students say each word. How are these words the same? (They have the same letters (vowels) inside.) Which letters are making the sound inside? (ou) Discuss the words in Group 2. How are these words the same? (They have the same sound at the end of each word.) Which letters are making the sound? (ow) What have you learned about the sounds that 'ou' and 'ow' make. (They make the same sound but the letters are different.) The 'ou' sound is usually heard inside the word while the 'ow' sound may be heard in the middle or at the end of a word.

Picture Key: Row 1: cow, cloud, mouse, owl Row 2: clown, blouse, flower, couch

Activity Worksheet: Page 118 **A.** The students will label each picture with the correct word. **B.** Students will complete the sentences with the missing words. **Answer Key: A.** Row 1: cow, cloud, mouse, owl Row 2: clown, blouse flower, couch **B.** 1. gown 2. crowd, shouted 3. bough 4. grouchy, frown 5. flour 6. proud, crown 7. mouse, mouth 8. sound, owl 9. clown, couch

Day 3: On a chart record the following words: blew, drew, new, grew. Have the students say the words and note how they end. What sound do you hear in all the words? (oo) Which letters are making that sound? (ew) The 'ew' sound is mainly heard at the end of a word. Record these words on the chart: food, tool, loop, shoot. Have the students say the words. What sound do you hear inside each word. (oo) Explain that the diphthong 'ew' is usually heard at the end of a word while the vowel digraph 'oo' is usually heard inside a word.

Activity Worksheet: Page 119 **A.** The students will complete each word with the correct sound. **B.** The students will match each word to its clue. **Answer Key: A.** 1. oo 2. ew 3. ew 4. oo 5. oo 6. ew or oo 7. oo 8. ew 9. ew 10. ew 11. oo 12. oo **B.** 1. cool 2. dew 3. root 4. chew 5. coop 6. roof 7. new 8. stew 9. hoop 10. room

Day 4: Review the diphthongs 'oi, oy, ou, aw, and ew.' On a chart record the incomplete words with the diphthongs. Across the top of the chart record the diphthongs 'oi, oy, ou, ow, ew.' Have the students complete the following exercise printed on the chart: 1. n __ se 2. h __ nd 3. sh __ er 4. enj __ 5. t __ 6. c __ nt 7. dr __ 8. c __ l 9. br __ 10. dr __ n _Possible Answers:_ 1. oi 2. ou 3. ow, 4, oy 5. oy 6.ou 7. ew 8. oi 9. ew 10. ow. Once the words are completed have the students say the words.

Activity Worksheet: Page 120 **A.** The students are to complete the sentences using the words in the word box. **Answer Key:** 1. loud, noise 2. royal, house 3. clown, powder 4. storm, destroy 5. boy, plowed, soil 6. owl, flew, brown 7. clay, round 8. clouds, about 9. bounced, down 10. chew

Day 5: Auditory and Visual Discrimination Test Page 121
A. Auditory Test: The students will circle the diphthong in each box heard in the word spoken by the teacher. **Words:** 1. coins 2. grew 3. scout 4. point 5. growl 6. threw 7. joy 8. threw
Answer Key: 1. oi 2. ew 3. ou 4. oi 5. ow 6. ew 7. oy 8. ew

B. Visual Discrimination Test: The students will record the word in brackets that completes each sentence. **Answer Key:** 1. ground 2. mouth 3. blew 4. boil 5. fountain 6. owl 7. house 8. drown 9. join 10. screw

Name: _____ Day 1 | Week 19

Remember: A **diphthong** is a sound made when **two** vowels blend together to make **one** sound.

The sounds '**oy**' and '**oi**' are called **diphthongs**

Examples: boy, enjoy, annoy   boil, join, noise

A. Use the diphthongs '**oi**' and '**oy**' to complete each word.

1. br ____ l
2. t ____
3. ann ____
4. p ____ nt
5. s ____ l
6. j ____ n
7. enj ____
8. r ____ al
9. c ____ n

B. Complete each sentence with the correct word found in the Word Box.

Word Box
| boy | coins | destroy | joint | joy |
| spoil | decoy | point | voice | annoy |

1. Frank's grandfather gave him five different _____ to save.

2. The wind during a bad storm can _____ trees and buildings.

3. A _____ is a place where bones are joined in our bodies.

4. The hunter placed a _____ in the water to get the wild ducks to come closer.

5. It is not polite to _____ your finger at someone.

6. The children shouted for _____ when school ended in June.

7. The young _____ loved to go fishing with his dad.

8. The girl had a beautiful singing _____.

9. Fruit must be kept in a cold place or it will _____.

10. The children who kept talking began to _____ their teacher.

Name: _____ Day 2 | Week 19

The letters 'ou' and 'ow' are called **diphthongs**.

In a word they make the same sound.

Examples: br**ow**n n**ow** d**ow**n   l**ou**d c**ou**nt s**ou**th

The '**ou**' sound is usually found **inside** a word. The '**ow**' sound is often found **inside** a word or at the **end** of a word.

A. Match these words to their pictures. Print them on the lines under the pictures.

> blouse   cow   couch   flower   cloud   owl   clown   mouse

B. Record these words in the sentences.

> clown   mouth   owl   shouted   flour
> sound   crown   crowd   gown   proud
> couch   grouchy   bough   frown   mouse

1. The princess was dressed in a beautiful pink ball _____.
2. The _____ _____ when their team won a gold medal.
3. The strong wind blew a _____ off the maple tree.
4. The _____ boy had a _____ on his face.
5. _____ is used to make many things that we eat.
6. The _____ prince wore a _____ on his head.
7. The _____ had a piece of cheese to put in its _____.
8. The _____ that you heard is an _____ hooting at night.
9. The _____ curled up on the _____ and fell asleep.

Name: _____   Day 3 | Week 19

Here is some news!

The letters '**ew**' are called a **diphthong** and are often found at the **end** of a root word.

The letters '**oo**' are called a **vowel digraph** and are often found **inside** a word.

The letters '**ew**' and '**oo**' make the same sound

A. Complete each word with the correct sound. Is it '**oo**' or '**ew?**'

1. g ____ se
2. bl ____
3. gr ____
4. f ____ d
5. h ____ p
6. m ____
7. c ____ l
8. dr ____
9. st ____
10. kn ____
11. r ____ m
12. t ____ th

B. Can you **spell** the answer to each clue?

1. It is the opposite to warm. _____

2. It makes the grass wet in the morning during the summer. _____

3. It holds a plant in the ground. _____

4. We do this to food with our teeth. _____

5. It is a home for chickens on a farm. _____

6. It is the top part of a house. _____

7. It is something not old. _____

8. It is meat and vegetables cooked together in a big pot. _____

9. It is a plastic circle you can get inside and spin. _____

10. It is a space found inside a house. _____

Name: _____ Day 4 | Week 19

Remember to use the sounds that '**ou, oy, ow, oi** and **ew**' make.

Examples: l<u>ou</u>d br<u>ow</u>n b<u>oy</u> c<u>oi</u>n fl<u>ew</u>

A. Use the words in the Word Box to complete the sentences.

Word Box				
house	powder	noise	storm	clown
destroy	boy	clay	royal	plowed
loud	owl	clouds	soil	chew
about	bounced	down	round	brown

1. There was a _____ banging _____ when the cars hit each other.

2. A _____ family lives in a _____ called a castle.

3. The _____ put white _____ all over his face.

4. A bad _____ may _____ houses in many towns and cities.

5. The _____ rode in his father's tractor while he _____ the _____ in the fields.

6. The _____ quickly flew after the little _____ rabbit.

7. The girl formed the _____ into a _____ ball.

8. The fluffy _____ sailed _____ the sky like puffy balls.

9. When the bus hit a bump the children _____ up and _____.

10. Some kids like to _____ bubble gum and blow big bubbles.

Name: _____   Day 5 | Week 19

Auditory and Visual Discrimination Test on the Diphthongs 'oi, oy, ou, ow, ew'

A. Auditory Test:

1. oy oi	2. ow ew	3. oy ou	4. oi ou
5. ow oy	6. ew ow	7. oy ow	8. ou ew

B. Visual Discrimination Test:

1. In the fall, the leaves fall onto the _____ . (ground, grown)

2. Eric fell down on the walk and hurt his _____. (month, mouth)

3. The rain poured down and the wind _____. (blow, blew)

4. My mother put the kettle on to _____ water to make some tea.
   (bowl, boil)

5. We threw some coins in the _____ and made a wish.
   (found, fountain)

6. The big _____ had large eyes and a short beak. (oil, owl)

7. My friend lives in a brick _____ across the street. (house, horse)

8. You can _____ in water if you cannot swim. (drown, down)

9. I want to _____ a hockey team. (joy, join)

10. You can use a _____ to fix the bike. (stew, screw)

Week 20: **Syllabication**

Objective: To make students aware that syllables in words may contain regular double vowels, irregular double vowels and diphthongs.

Day 1: On a chart record the following group of words: join, stew, south, toy, how. Have the students say the words, underline the diphthong or the irregular double vowel in each one. Have them tell the number of syllables that they hear in each word. Discuss the number of vowel sounds heard and why the words only have one syllable. Record these words on the chart: reindeer, feather, wooden, autumn, royal. Have the students say and clap each word. How many syllables are in each word. (2) Which words have a double vowel sound that is not a regular one? (reindeer, feather, autumn, royal) Have the students underline the irregular double vowel sound in each word. (ei, ea, au, oy) Which word has a regular and irregular double vowel sound? (reindeer) Which double vowel is it? (ee) Words with more than one syllable or word part can have regular and irregular double vowels.

Activity Worksheet: Page 123 **A.** The students will complete the chart. **Answer Key:** 1. ea, I, 1 2. ai, R, 2 3. ei, ee, R, I, 2 4. au, u, R, I, 2 5. ea, I, 1 6. ea, a, I, 2 7. ei, ee, R, I, 2 8. oo, I, 1 8. oo, I, 1 9. oo, ie, I, 2 10. ea, I, 1

Day 2: Review the recognition of syllables in words containing irregular and regular double vowels. Record the following words down a chart: spool, annoy, enjoy, mouth, toenail, window, fountain. Beside each word record the vowel sounds heard and the number of syllables. Example: breakfast, ea, a, 2

Activity Worksheet: Page 124 **A.** The students are to record the number of vowels they see, vowels sounds they hear and the number of syllables in each word on the chart. **Answer Key: A.** 2, 1, 1 **B.** 3, 2, 2 **C.** 2, 1, 1 **D.** 3, 2, 2 **E.** 2, 1, 1 **F.** 2, 2, 2 **G.** 2, 1, 1 **H.** 2, 2, 2 **I.** 2, 1, 1 **J.** 3, 2, 2 **K.** 2, 1, 1 **L.** 3, 1, 1 **M.** 2, 2, 2 **N.** 2, 1, 1 **O.** 2, 2, 2 **P.** 2, 2, 2 **Q.** 2, 2, 2 **R.** 4, 2, 2 **S.** 3, 1, 1 **T.** 3, 2, 2 **U.** 2, 2, 2 **V.** 2, 2, 2 **W.** 2, 2, 2 **X.** 2, 1, 1

Day 3: Review the number of syllables in words containing irregular double vowels. Record the following words down one side of a chart. **Words:** 1. robin 2. spool 3. blouse 4. steal 5. autumn 6. between 7. napkin 8. cowboy 9. broomstick 10. airplane. Have the students say each word and tell how many vowels that they see and hear in each word. **Answers:** 1. 2, short o, i 2. 1, oo 3. 1, ou 4. 1, ea 5. 2, au, u 6. 3, long e, ee 7. 2, short a, short i 8. 2. ow, oy 9. 2, oo, short i 10. 2, ai, a

Activity Worksheet: Page 125 **A.** The students are to record the vowel(s) seen, heard and the number of syllables in each word. **Answer Key:** Row 1: spool - 2, 1, 1; cloudy - 3, 2, 2; joyful - 3, 2, 2; toybox - 3, 2, 2; mouth - 2, 1, 1 raccoon - 3, 2, 2; doctor - 2, 2, 2; elephant - 3, 3, 3; tooth - 2, 1, 1; baseball - 3, 2, 2; cherry - 2, 2, 2; ghost - 1, 1, 1: Row 2: broom - 2, 1,1; raccoon - 3, 2, 2; goose - 3, 1,1; voice: 3, 1, 1; angry - 2, 2, 2; snake - 2, 1, 1; church - 1, 1, 1; dragon - 2, 2, 2; potato - 3, 3, 3; camel - 2, 2, 2; gold - 1, 1, 1; squeaky - 3, 2, 2

Day 4: Review the number of vowel sounds and syllables in words. Have the students listen to each word that you say and have them tell the vowel sounds that they hear and the number of syllables in each one. **Words:** found (ou, 1); autumn (au, u, 2); coat (oa, 1); sheep (ee, 1); neatness (ea, e, 2); boathouse (oa, ou, 2); pumpkin (u, i, 2); golden (o, e, 2); umbrella (u, e, a, 3)

Activity Worksheet: Page 126 **A.** The students are to locate one, two and three syllable words in the Word Search using three different colours. **Answer Key:** One Syllable Words: broom, school, south, witch, clown, wood; Circled in red. Two Syllable Words: flowers, reindeer, cookie, mousetrap, rabbit, fountain; Circled in green. Three Syllable Words: strawberry, newspaper, woodpecker, umbrella, magician, chocolate; Circled in blue.

Day 5: Auditory and Visual Discrimination Test on Syllables in Words: Page 127
Auditory Test: The students are to circle the number of syllables heard in each word spoken by the teacher. **Words:** 1. mountain 2. possible 3. because 4. umbrella 5. spider 6. magician 7. trout 8. telephone 9. radio 10. crown **Answer Key:** 1. (2) 2. (3) 3. (2) 4. (3) 5. (2) 6. (3) 7. (1) 8. (3) 9. (3) 10. (1)
Visual Discrimination Test: The students will read the clues and record the answer found in the Word Box on the line. **Answer Key:** 1. crumble 2. crocodile 3. growl 4. cranberries 5. dragon 6. bee 7. cradle 8. clean 9. trumpet 10. whisper

Name: _____   Day 1 | Week 20

Remember!

Syllables are word parts. In each syllable there may be an irregular vowel sound.

Examples: bl**ow**, st**ew**, n**eigh**bour

Complete the chart below. Record the double vowel sound(s) heard in each word on the line. Record 'R' if it is a **regular** vowel sound or 'I' if it is an **irregular** vowel sound. Record the number of syllables that you hear in each word.

Word	Vowel Sounds	Regular	Irregular	Syllables
1. bread				
2. painted				
3. reindeer				
4. autumn				
5. thread				
6. breakfast				
7. reindeer				
8. goose				
9. cookies				
10. thread				

Name: _____   Day 2 | Week 20

Remember !

Each syllable in a word has a **vowel sound** that you can **see** and **hear**.

Example: In the word 'cookie' you can see four vowels, hear two vowels and the word has two syllables.

Each syllable in a word has a vowel sound.

A. Read each word.
   Record the number of vowels that you see,
      the number of vowels that you hear
               and
      the number of syllables in each word
      on the chart.

Words	Vowels Seen	Vowels Heard	Syllables	Words	Vowels Seen	Vowels Heard	Syllables
A. bread	___	___	___	M. funny	___	___	___
B. sweater	___	___	___	N. bone	___	___	___
C. school	___	___	___	O. dollar	___	___	___
D. raccoon	___	___	___	P. jigsaw	___	___	___
E. cloud	___	___	___	Q. cherry	___	___	___
F. flower	___	___	___	R. woodpile	___	___	___
G. grouch	___	___	___	S. goose	___	___	___
H. berry	___	___	___	T. cloudy	___	___	___
I. coin	___	___	___	U. rabbit	___	___	___
J. noisy	___	___	___	V. berry	___	___	___
K. cheek	___	___	___	W. pumpkin	___	___	___
L. cheese	___	___	___	X. tool	___	___	___

Name: _____   Day 3 | Week 20

One vowel sound = one syllable

In some words you may hear only **one vowel** sound. That word will have only **one syllable**.

If you hear more than one vowel sound in a word it may have two or more syllables.

Examples: stew (1), powder (2), newspaper (3)

On the lines in the chart, record the number of vowels that you see and hear and the number of syllables in each word.

Words	Vowels I see	Vowels I hear	Syllables	Words	Vowels I see	Vowels I hear	Syllables
spool	___	___	___	broom	___	___	___
cloudy	___	___	___	raccoon	___	___	___
joyful	___	___	___	goose	___	___	___
toybox	___	___	___	voice	___	___	___
mouth	___	___	___	angry	___	___	___
raccoon	___	___	___	snake	___	___	___
doctor	___	___	___	church	___	___	___
elephant	___	___	___	dragon	___	___	___
tooth	___	___	___	potato	___	___	___
baseball	___	___	___	camel	___	___	___
cherry	___	___	___	gold	___	___	___
ghost	___	___	___	squeaky	___	___	___

Name: _____ Day 4 | Week 20

Words may have one, two or three or more syllables.

Examples: pep   pepper   peppermint

A. Search for words in the Word Search that have one, two or three syllables.

   Colour **one** syllable words **red**.

   Colour **two** syllable words **green**.

   Colour **three** syllable words **blue**.

```
u o r f s e g f a g z y h y i x j w k v l u m t n s o r
n f l o w e r s t s c b r o o m p z d c c l o w n e f g
w h p u x y z o u t y d e z b x y a w b t x y z a c b d
r s t n a w y u e u x x i z a w b c m a g i c i a n u v
e f g t p b x t f v t w n e w s p a p e r q r n o p m l
c r q a o n e h z v s w d n a c l k l m n p w i t c h r
k d j i l m a d n i k j e j l h m d f e o j o k l m n a
h m i n c e d b e d f g e t s o b n o g f b o z a y w b
f o g e n b a q z f y x r v u o q m u n o p d o q t u b
x u w m v o p u r s g t w k r l n o n p k l p b p r d i
a s t r a w b e r r y h q r s j t u t v w x e y z c g t
v e b i r p j k a o n k l i m q i r a s d t c o o k i e
u t l c m n q o b p j l m j q g r h i s t u k e v w x y
h r w e d v u m b r e l l a k a c e n y a m e h f l l j
j a m n o z p u v a t s h b r g f o n h o i r l m j h k
c p d e m a r s n x y z t a d c h o c o l a t e x y z a
```

Name: _____   Day 5 | Week 20

Auditory and Visual Discrimination Test on Syllabication

A. Auditory Test:

1. 1 2 3	2. 1 2 3	3. 1 2 3	4. 1 2 3	5. 1 2 3
6. 1 2 3	7. 1 2 3	8. 1 2 3	9. 1 2 3	10. 1 2 3

B. Visual Discrimination Test:

| whisper | trumpet | clean | cradle | bee |
| crumble | crocodile | dragon | cranberries | growl |

1. Which two syllable word means to fall apart? _____

2. Which three syllable word is an animal that lives in a swamp?
   _____

3. Which one syllable word tells what animals do when they are angry?
   _____

4. Which three syllable word is a fruit served with turkey?
   _____

5. Which two syllable word is a storybook creature that breathes fire?
   _____

6. Which one syllable words is an insect that stings? _____

7. Which two syllable word is a bed for a baby? _____

8. Which one syllable word is the opposite to dirty? _____

9. Which two syllable word is used to play music? _____

10. Which two syllable word means to talk softly? _____

Week 21: Consonant Digraphs

Objective: To make students aware of the sounds made by the consonant digraphs 'sh, ch, wh, th, ck, kn, ph, gn, wr, gh.'

Day 1: On a chart record the following words: shirt, chair, whip, thin, pheasant, kick, know, sign, write, high. Have the students circle the two consonants in each word that are making one sound together. Explain to your students that two consonants together in a word often make one sound. They are called consonant digraphs.

Picture Key: Row 1: cheese, knee, thief, phone, knife, Row 2: wreath, sign, laugh, shell, whale

Activity Worksheet: Page 129 **A.** The students will record the consonant digraph heard in each picture on the line. **B.** The students will circle the consonant digraph seen and heard in each word. **Answer Key: A:** Row 1: ch, kn, th, ph, kn Row 2: wr, gn, gh, sh, wh **B:** Row 1: gh, wr, ph, sh, wh, kn, ch Row 2: ck, gh, wh, ph, ch, sh, kn Row 3: th, gn, ck, ck, gh, ck, ph

Day 2: Review the consonant digraphs with this exercise. On a chart record the following sounds across the top: sh, th, ch, wh, ck, kn, ph, gn, wr, gh. Under the sounds record the following incomplete words: 1. bir(th)day 2. tele(ph)one 3. (ch)oke 4. (wr)ist 5. rou(gh) 6. bru(sh) 7. thr(ew) 8. ni(ck)el 9. (kn)ot 10. (wh)isper. Have the students complete each word with a consonant digraph.

Activity Worksheet: Page 130 **A.** The students will complete the sentences with words from the Word Box. **Answer Key:** 1. wren 2. whistle 3. gnaw 4. elephant 5. knit 6. shout 7. wrench 8. cough 9. sign 10. knock

Day 3: On a chart record the following group of words: beach, path, dishes, whine, tooth, wrist, tough, chin, show, wheat, laugh, phone, knot. Have a student say the word and circle the consonant digraph in it. Use the same procedure for the rest of the words.

Activity Worksheet: Page 131 **A.** The students will complete each word with a consonant digraph. **Answer Key: A.** 1. wh 2. kn 3. th 4. gh 5. sh 6. wr 7. ch 8. ck 9. kn 10. ph 11. gn 12. kn **B.** The students will use the completed words to finish each sentence. **Answer Key:** 1. knot 2. write 3. phone 4. kneel 5. signs 6. tickets 7. wheel 8. brush 9. knocked 10. chin 11. cough 12. truth

Day 4: Review the following consonant digraphs: ph, kn, wr, gh, ch, gn. Record the digraphs at the top of the chart. Beneath the digraphs record the following incomplete words. Have the students choose the digraph at the top of the chart that will complete each word. Words: 1. lau __ (gh) 2. __ ong (wr) 3. __ ow (kn) 4. cou __ (gh) 5. __ aw (gn) 6. __ ite (wr) 7. dol __ hin (ph) 8. __ oto (ph) 9. rou __ (gh) 10. mar__ (ch) Once the activity is completed have the students read the words aloud.

Activity Worksheet: Page 132 **A.** The students will complete the unfinished word in each sentence with a digraph. **Answer Key:** 1. kn 2. wr 3. ph 4. ch 5. kn 6. gn 7. wr 8. ph 9. wr 10. wr 11. kn 12. gh

Day 5: Auditory and Visual Discrimination Test on the Consonant Digraphs 'sh, ch, wh, th, ck, kn, ph, gn, wr, gh' Page 133

Auditory Test: The students are to listen carefully to each word that the teacher says and then circle the consonant digraph heard in it. **Words:** 1. choke 2. write 3. cluck 4. rough 5. bushel 6. teeth 7. wheat 8. knife 9. pheasant 10. sign **Answer Key:** 1. ch 2. wr 3. ck 4. gh 5. sh 6. th 7. wh 8. kn 9. ph 10. gn

Visual Discrimination Test: The students will classify each word in the lists as to the position the digraph has in each one. Is it found at the beginning, the middle, or at the end of each word?
Answer Key: <u>Beginning:</u> whine, knife, show, know, gnaw, chin, wrong, write <u>Middle:</u> dishes, peaches, telephone, another, teacher, elephant, kitchen, birthday <u>End:</u> beach, ranch, tooth, brush, sign, tough, wrist, patch

Name: _____   Day 1 | Week 21

Some sounds work as a team!

Did you know that some consonants form a **team** and make **one** sound together.

They are called **consonant digraphs**.

Consonant digraphs are 'sh, th, wh, ch, ck, kn, ph, gn, wr, gh.'

They may be found at the <u>beginning</u>, <u>middle</u> or <u>end</u> of a word.

A. Print the missing consonant digraph in each picture's name.

___ eese   ___ ee   ___ ief   ___ one   ___ ife

___ eath   si ___   lau ___   ___ ell   ___ ale

B. Circle each **consonant digraph** that you see in each word.

Row 1	Row 2	Row 3
tough	cluck	beneath
write	rough	gnaw
elephant	wheel	ticket
brush	dolphin	trick
whip	choke	cough
knot	bush	neck
patch	knit	graph

Name: _____ Day 2 | Week 21

Consonant digraphs are found at the **beginning, middle** and **end** of words.

Consonant digraphs are '**sh, ch, th, wh, ck, kn, gn, wr** and **gh**.'

Look at the beginning, middle and end of a word.

A. Use the words in the Word Box to complete the following sentences.

Word Box				
elephant	wren	shout	wrench	cough
whistle	gnaw	sign	knock	knit

1. A _____ is a very tiny brown bird.

2. The police officer blew his _____ to get the cars to stop.

3. Beavers like to _____ at the trunks of trees.

4. The largest animal at the zoo was a big grey _____.

5. My mother likes to _____ sweaters and mittens for us to wear.

6. Out teacher does not _____ at her pupils.

7. The plummer fixed the pipe with a _____ from his tool box.

8. Tim had a cold with a bad _____.

9. The _____ at the corner told everyone to stop.

10. Did you hear someone _____ at the front door.

Name: _____   Day 3 | Week 21

Where are consonant digraphs found?

Consonant digraphs are found at the **beginning**, **middle** or at the **end** of words.

Examples: kitchen   laugh   know

A. Use the following consonant digraphs in the box to complete the words.

| sh | th | wh | ch | ck | kn | ph | gn | wr | gh |

1. ____ eel
2. ____ ocked
3. tru ____
4. cou ____
5. bru ____
6. ____ ite
7. ____ in
8. ti ____ ets
9. ____ eel
10. ____ one
11. si ____ s
12. ____ ot

B. Use each word that you completed in the correct sentence.

1. The sailor tied a _____ in the thick rope to hold the boat in place.
2. I _____ letters to a friend who lives in Nunavut.
3. You should not use your cell _____ while you are driving.
4. People must _____ when they come before Queen Elizabeth.
5. People who cannot hear make _____ with their hands.
6. We have _____ to see the next Bluejay baseball game.
7. The _____ on the wagon got stuck in a big muddy hole.
8. I went to the barn to _____ my horse.
9. Someone _____ on our door late last night.
10. The old man had long whiskers on his _____.
11. Always cover your mouth when you _____ or sneeze.
12. People should always tell the _____ and not lie.

Name: _____   Day 4 | Week 21

Digraphs may be found at the <u>beginning</u>, in the <u>middle</u> and at the <u>end</u> of words.

Examples: go**ph**er **kn**ob **wr**ong trou**gh** mu**ch** si**gn**

Where do I look for digraphs?

A. Use the **digraphs** in the Sound Box to complete the unfinished word in each sentence.

Sound Box					
ph	kn	wr	gh	ch	gn

1. Dad used a sharp ____ife to carve the face of a jack-o'-lantern on the pumpkin.

2. The little earthworm ____iggled away quickly to hide from the robin.

3. I know how to print all the letters of the al____abet.

4. My brother and I enjoy playing the game called ____eckers.

5. Each finger on you hands has a ____uckle that bends.

6. On the door of the shop was a si ____ that said closed.

7. At Christmas we hang a ____eathe on our door.

8. A go ____ er likes to live in a hole on the prairies in Saskatchewan.

9. Billy wanted a ____ ist watch for a birthday present.

10. The boys will ____estle on mats in the gym.

11. Janice did not ____ow how hard it was raining outside.

12. We had a good lau ____ when Terry told his funny joke.

Name: _____   Day 5 | Week 21

Auditory and Visual Discrimination Test on the Consonant Digraphs 'sh, ch, th, wh, ck, kn, ph, gn, wr, gh'

A. Auditory Test:

1. sh ch ck	2. wh wr ck	3. ck gn ch	4. ch ph gh	5. ch th sh
6. wr th ck	7. wr wh th	8. ck kn ph	9. ch sh ph	10. kn gh gn

B. Visual Discrimination Test:

beach	peaches	know	teacher	write	birthday
dishes	telephone	show	brush	sign	patch
whine	another	tooth	chin	tough	wrist
knife	ranch	gnaw	wrong	elephant	kitchen

Beginning	Middle	End
_____	_____	_____
_____	_____	_____
_____	_____	_____
_____	_____	_____
_____	_____	_____
_____	_____	_____
_____	_____	_____
_____	_____	_____

Week 22: Recognition of Prefixes

Objective: To make students aware that words may begin with the prefixes 'un, dis, ex, de, re'

Day 1: On a chart record the following words: disappear, disobey, dislike, disagree. Discuss the words: How are these words the same? (They all begin with the same three letters.) What are the names of the letters? (d, i, s) These letters form a prefix that is a syllable. It is found at the beginning of a word and is used before a root word to change its meaning or to make a new word. Record the following words on the chart: unfair, unfold, uncertain, undo. Discuss the words. How are these words the same? (They all begin with the same two letters.) What are their names? (u, n) The letters 'un' form a prefix. The prefixes 'dis' and 'un' mean 'not.'

Activity Worksheet: Page 135 **A.** The students are to record the prefix 'un' or 'dis' at the beginning of each root word. **B.** The students are to use the words they made in the sentences. **Answer Key: A.** 1. un 2. dis 3. un 4. dis 5. un 6. dis 7. un or dis 8. dis 9. un 10. dis 11. un 12. dis **B.** 1. unscrew 2. dislike 3. displeased 4. unfold 5. disobey 6. unsafe 7. uncover 8. disorder 9. unable 10. discovered 11. disappeared 12. unchain

Day 2: Record the following words on a chart: disobey, unfold, distrust, unchain, unable, disliked. Have the students say the words. Have them circle the prefix and underline the root word in each one. Discuss their meanings. Which word means: 1. not to like (dislikes) 2. can't do something (unable) 3. doesn't trust (distrust) 4. not liked (disliked) 5. doesn't do as they are told (disobey) 6. to undo something (unfold)

Activity Worksheet: Page 136 **A.** Record the root word for each word on the line. **B.** Use the words in the Word Box to complete each sentence. **Answer Key: A.** 1. fair 2. pin 3. appear 4. true 5. like 6. safe 7. obey 8. hurt 9. please 10. load **B.** 1. unsafe 2. disorder 3. unload 4. unlock 5. disobey 6. disarm 7. untrue 8. unpleasant 9. untie

Day 3: Introduce the prefixes '**re, de,** and **ex**' to your students. Record the following words on the chart: **Group 1** - repair, redo, rewrap, refill **Group 2** - derail, depart, defrost, delight **Group 3** - exchange, express, excuse, expect, explain. Have your students read Group 1 words. Have them circle the prefix and underline the root word. Explain that the prefix '**re**' means '**to do again**.' Discuss Group 2 words. Circle the prefix and underline the root word. Explain that the prefix '**de**' means '**from**'. Discuss Group 3 words. Circle the prefix and underline the root word. Explain that the prefix '**ex**' means '**out of**' or '**from**.'

Activity Worksheet: Page 137 **A.** Record the prefix and root word on the lines beside each word. **Answer Key:** 1. re - read 2. de - frost 3. re - trace 4. dis - please 5. un - pin 6. dis - obey 7. un - safe 8. re - read 9. un - do 10. ex - press 11. un - happy 12. de - part 13. re - heat 14. un - able 15. re - fill 16. un - wrap 17. de - rail 18. ex - plain 19. de - tour 20. un - kind

Day 4: Review the prefixes 'ex, de, and re.' Record the following words on a chart: 1. disobey 2. rebuild 3. derail 4. rewash 5. refill 6. displease 7. dislike 8. unsafe 9. discharge 10. unload. Have the students locate the word that matches the following meanings said by the teacher: **Meanings** - 1. to let go (discharge) 2. dangerous (unsafe) 3. broke a rule (disobey) 4. run off the tracks (derail) 5. to make over again (rebuild) 6. to make someone unhappy (displease) 7. to make clean again (rewash) 8. does not care for it (dislike) 9. to remove from a vehicle (unload) 10. to make full again (refill)

Activity Worksheet: Page 138 **A.** The students will complete each sentence using the words from the Word Box. **Answer Key:** 1. disobey 2. reread 3. dislike 4. expert 5. rewrite 6. reheat 7. dishonest 8. defrost 9. explore 10. rebuild 11. unfair 12. exchange

Day 5: Auditory and Visual Discrimination Test on the Prefixes 'un, dis, er, de, re' Page 139
A. Auditory Test: The students are to listen to each word the teacher says and then circle the prefix heard at its beginning. **Words:** 1. depress 2. dislike 3. retell 4. untie 5. exchange 6. redo 7. unhappy 8. disappear **Answer Key:** 1. de 2. dis 3. re 4. un 5. ex 6. re 7. un 8. dis

B. Visual Discrimination Test: The students will complete each sentence with the correct word found in the Word Box. **Answer Key:** 1. dislike 2. refill 3. detour 4. depart 5. explore 6. exchange 7. dishonest 8. disappear 9. redo 10. reopen 11. unwrap 12. unable

Name: _____   Day 1 | Week 22

Remember this rule!

A **prefix** is a **syllable** placed before a root word to change its meaning or to make a new word.

Examples: '*unhappy*' means not happy

'*dislike*' means not to like

A. Record the prefix '**un**' or '**dis**' at the beginning of each word.

1. _____ fold
2. _____ obey
3. _____ safe
4. _____ appeared
5. _____ chain
6. _____ pleased
7. _____ cover
8. _____ like
9. _____ able
10. _____ covered
11. _____ screw
12. _____ order

B. Use the words that you made using the prefixes in the following sentences.

1. Can you _____ this lid from this jar of jam.

2. I _____ mustard being put on my ham sandwiches.

3. Lisa's report card _____ her mother and her father.

4. Please _____ the blanket and lay it on the grass.

5. It is wrong to _____ the people who care for you.

6. It is _____ to walk alone late at night.

7. Help me to _____ the boat so we can go for a ride in it.

8. The teacher did not like _____ in her classroom.

9. The boy using crutches was _____ to walk far.

10. Newfoundland was _____ by the Vikings many years ago.

11. The little ghost _____ when he saw the men in the house.

12. Please _____ your dog and take it for a walk.

Name: _____   Day 2 | Week 22

Remember!

A **prefix** is a syllable placed in front of a root word to make a new word.

Example: **un**fair   **dis**honest

A. Record each root word on the line beside each word.

1. unfair _____   6. unsafe _____

2. unpin _____   7. disobey _____

3. disappear _____ 8. unhurt _____

4. untrue _____   9. displease _____

5. dislike _____   10. unload _____

B. Complete each sentence with a word from the Word Box.

Word Box
untie	unpleasant	disarm
disobey	unload	unsafe
disorder	unlock	untrue

1. It is _____ to skate on a pond with thin ice.

2. Terry left his bedroom messy and in _____.

3. Will you help me _____ the dishwasher.

4. Please _____ the door for me with this key.

5. It is not wise to _____ the laws in Canada.

6. The police officer had to _____ the robber who had a gun.

7. The story the boy told about seeing a bear was _____.

8. A skunk's spray is very _____ to smell.

9. Please _____ your running shoes before you take them off.

Name: _____   Day 3 | Week 22

Don't forget the meaning of these **prefixes**!

The prefix '**re**' usually means 'to do again.'

Examples: rewrite - means 'to write again'

The prefix '**de**' usually means 'to go away from'

Example: depart means 'to go away from a place'

The prefix '**ex**' means 'out of' or 'from.'

Example: export means 'to send out of'

A. Record the prefix and the root word on the lines beside each word.

1. reread   _____ _____
2. defrost   _____ _____
3. retrace   _____ _____
4. displease   _____ _____
5. unpin   _____ _____
6. disobey   _____ _____
7. unsafe   _____ _____
8. reread   _____ _____
9. undo   _____ _____
10. express   _____ _____

11. unhappy   _____ _____
12. depart   _____ _____
13. reheat   _____ _____
14. unable   _____ _____
15. refill   _____ _____
16. unwrap   _____ _____
17. derail   _____ _____
18. explain   _____ _____
19. detour   _____ _____
20. unkind   _____ _____

Name: _____   Day 4 | Week 22

Remember the prefixes '**ex**, **de** and **re**' can change the **meanings** of root words.

Examples: <u>re</u>paint means to paint again; <u>de</u>part means to go away from; <u>ex</u>cite means to cause a feeling

A. Complete each sentence using the words from the Word Box.

Word Box			
dishonest	explore	expert	reread
rewrite	reheat	rebuild	dislike
exchange	defrost	disobey	unfair

1. You should never _____ your parents.

2. I had to _____ the story to find out the answers to the questions.

3. The players on the baseball team _____ their captain.

4. Kim and Sharon are _____ soccer players.

5. David lost his finished homework and had to _____ it again.

6. Rami was late getting home and had to _____ his supper.

7. Someone who cheats or steals is a _____ person.

8. The new refrigerator is able to _____ itself.

9. The two men set out to _____ the inside of the cave that they found.

10. Exercising at a gym helps to _____ your muscles.

11. The coach of Mark's hockey team is _____ to the players.

12. I took my new sweaters back to the store to _____ them for a bigger size.

Name: _____   Day 5 | Week 22

Auditory and Visual Discrimination Test on the Prefixes 'in, dis, er, de, re'

A. Auditory Test:

1. dis de ex	2. de re dis	3. un de re	4. dis un re
5. re ex de	6. ex re de	7. ex un de	8. dis de re

B. Visual Discrimination Test:

explore   unwrap   dislike   refill   depart   redo
exchange   reopen   disappear   detour   dishonest   unable

1. I _____ having to go to bed early every night.

2. Jack will _____ his gas tank before he leaves for the city.

3. When a highway is being built cars often have to take a _____.

4. The plane we are taking will _____ from the airport at six o'clock.

5. It is fun to _____ the many lakes and rivers in Canada.

6. At Christmas, people in Canada like to _____ presents.

7. A person who tells lies all the time is very _____.

8. A magician likes to make things _____ .

9. I cannot read your writing so you will have to _____ it.

10. The store that had a fire will _____ soon.

11. You may _____ your presents now.

12. The boy was _____ to open the window without help.

Week 23: Prefixes, Root Words, Suffixes

Objective: To develop and strengthen the recognition of words that contain prefixes, root words and suffixes.

Day 1: Down a chart, record the following words: explaining, unfolding, displays, replaced, rebuilding, unscrewed, displaying, unscrewing. Have the students underline each root word, circle each prefix and box each suffix. Review the meaning of prefix, root word and suffix.

Activity Worksheet: Page 141 **A.** The students are to classify the parts of each word under the headings prefix, root word, and suffix **Answer Key:** 1. re - paint - ing 2. dis - pleas - ing 3. un - lock - ed 4. dis - play - ing 5. ex - plain - ed 6. de - tour - s 7. un - dress - ing 8. de - rail - ed 9. re - write - s 10. un - pack - ed 11. dis - obey - ed 12. un - cover - ing

Day 2: Review the prefixes 'un' and 'dis'. On a chart record the following root words: 1. ___ pleasure 2. ___ safe 3. ___ appear 4. ___ cover 5. ___ loading 6. ___ obey 7. ___ seen 8. ___ agree 9. ___ tied 10. ___ even Have the students change the meaning of the word using the prefixes 'un' and 'dis.'

Activity Worksheet: Page 142 **A.** The students are to complete each sentence with a word from the Word Box. **Answer Key:** 1. disappear 2. disobey 3. unpleasant 4. displeased 5. uneven 6. discovered 7. uncover 8. dislike 9. unhappy `10. untie 11. uncertain 12. unfair

Day 3: Review syllables in words containing suffixes. Record the following words on a chart. **Words:** spoonful, boneless, colder, warmest, lonely, helpless, kindness, reading, slower, sweeter. Have the students underline the root word and circle the suffix in each word. Remind your students that a suffix is a syllable if it contains a vowel.

Activity Worksheet: Page 143 **A.** The students are to separate the root word and the suffix with a hyphen. **B.** The students are to add a suffix to a root word that will form a word to complete each sentence. **Answer Key: A.** 1. loud-est 2. fly-ing 3. kind-ly 4. read-ing 5. help-less 6. care-less 7. play-ful 8. box-es 9. cold-er 10. turn-ing **B.** 1. kindness 2. friendly 3. careful 4. safely 5. playing 6. warmer 7. sadly 8. loudest 9. rested 10. helpless

Day 4: Review syllables in words that contain prefixes and suffixes. On a chart record the following words: painted, greener, unwilling, unpacking, looking, renew, spoonful, remaining, helpful. Have the students clap each word when said and separate the prefix, root word and the suffix with a hyphen. (-)

Activity Worksheet: Page 144 **A.** The students are to divide each word into syllables using hyphens. **Answer Key:** 1. play-ing 2. harm-ful 3. re-tell 4. un-will-ing 5. sweet-er 6. un-pack-ing 7. help-ful 8. de-rail 9. float-ing 10. un-paint-ed 11. re-turn-ing 12. quick-ly 13. de-feat-ed 14. green-er 15. in-vent-ed 16. sad-ly 17. un-kind-ly 18. re-main-ing 19. soft-er 20. ex-press

Day 5: Auditory and Visual Discrimination Test of Words With Syllables Page 145

A. Auditory Test: The students will circle the number that represents the number of syllables in each word said by the teacher. **Words:** 1. handful 2. paint 3. invented 4. express 5. displaying 6. untie 7. undressing 8. repairing Answer Key: 1. (2) 2. (1) 3. (3) 4. (2) 5. (3) 6. (2) 7. (3) 8. (3)

B: Visual Discrimination Test: The students are to read each sentence carefully and circle each word that has a prefix, suffix or both. On the line, at the end of the sentence, the students are to use hyphen(s) to separate the word into syllables. **Answer Key:** 1. re-turn 2. float-ed 3. un-pack-ing 4. swift-ly 5. re-sharp- en 6. rest-less 7. re-paint-ed 8. sweet-en 9. in-vent-ed 10. great-est

Name: _____ Day 1 | Week 23

Here are three more things to remember!

1. A **prefix** is a syllable put before a root word to change its meaning.

2. A **root word** is the word that may have a prefix or a suffix added to it to change its meaning.

3. A **suffix** is a letter or syllable placed at the end of a root word to change its meaning.

A. On the lines beside each word record the prefix, the root word and the suffix

Word	Prefix	Root Word	Suffix
1. repainting	_____	_____	_____
2. displeasing	_____	_____	_____
3. unlocked	_____	_____	_____
4. displaying	_____	_____	_____
5. explained	_____	_____	_____
6. detours	_____	_____	_____
7. undressing	_____	_____	_____
8. derailed	_____	_____	_____
9. rewrites	_____	_____	_____
10. unpacked	_____	_____	_____
11. disobeyed	_____	_____	_____
12. uncovering	_____	_____	_____

Name: _____ Day 2 | Week 23

Remember! A **prefix** is a syllable placed before a root word.
It often changes the meaning of the word or makes a new word.
The prefixes '**un**' and '**dis**' mean '**not**'.

Examples: **Dishonest** mean not honest.
Unfair means not fair

A. Use the words in the Word Box to complete the following sentences.

Word Box

unpleasant	disobey	disappear	uncover
unhappy	dislike	untie	uncertain
unfair	displeased	uneven	discovered

1. The hot sun made the snow quickly _____.

2. Children should not _____ their parents.

3. A garbage pail often has an _____ smell.

4. Yannik's dad was _____ when he read his son's report card.

5. The boards on the kitchen floor were _____ and squeaked.

6. A French explorer _____ Newfoundland on one of his trips.

7. Help me _____ the pool so we can go swimming.

8. I _____ eating toast covered with honey.

9. Maria was very _____ when she was told she could not go to the movies.

10. Make sure you _____ your shoes before you take them off.

11. The man was _____ about which street to take.

12. It is _____ to cheat while playing a game.

Name: _____   Day 3 | Week 23

A **suffix** is a syllable if it contains a **vowel sound**.

Examples: sleepless   newest   sadly

A. Separate each word into syllables using a hyphen (-).

1. loudest _____   6. careless _____
2. flying   _____   7. playful   _____
3. kindly   _____   8. boxes   _____
4. reading _____   9. colder   _____
5. helpless _____   10. turning _____

B. Add a **suffix** to each **root word** to make a word to complete each sentence.

Suffixes: ly, ness, ful, ing, er, est, ed, less

Root Words: loud, sad, warm, play, kind, friend, care, safe, rest, help

1. The old lady thanked the girl for her _____.
2. The children in the class were _____ to the new girl.
3. We should always be _____ when we spend money.
4. Always cross busy streets _____.
5. The boys were _____ baseball at the park.
6. In the summer the sun is _____.
7. The boy who lost the race walked away _____.
8. The smallest boy in the class had the _____ voice.
9. The sick boy _____ all afternoon in his bed.
10. The man stood _____ as he watched the plane crash onto the ground.

Name: _____   Day 4 | Week 23

Remember !

A **suffix** is a **syllable** if it contains a **vowel sound**.

Examples: fear**less**   new**est**   walk**ing**

A **prefix** is a **syllable** in itself.

Examples: **re**turn   **un**safe   **dis**like

A. Separate the words into syllables using hyphens (-) on the lines.

Example: unwilling   -   un - will - ing

1. playing _____
2. harmful _____
3. retell _____
4. unwilling _____
5. sweeter _____
6. unpacking _____
7. helpful _____
8. derail _____
9. floating _____
10. unpainted _____

11. returning _____
12. quickly _____
13. defeated _____
14. greener _____
15. invented _____
16. sadly _____
17. unkindly _____
18. remaining _____
19. softer _____
20. express _____

Name: _____   Day 5 | Week 23

Auditory and Visual Discrimination Test on Words With Syllables

A. Auditory Test:

1.	2.	3.	4.
1 2 3	1 2 3	1 2 3	1 2 3
5.	6.	7.	8.
1 2 3	1 2 3	1 2 3	1 2 3

B. Visual Discrimination Test:

1. Please return this book to the library. _____

2. We floated down the river on a raft. _____

3. Maggie was busy unpacking her suitcase. _____

4. The ambulance driver drove swiftly to the hospital. _____

5. I have to get someone to resharpen my hockey skates. _____

6. The people became very restless while they stood in line. _____

7. The fence around the barn needed to be repainted. _____

8. Use some brown sugar to sweeten your porridge. _____

9. Alexander Bell was the man who invented the telephone. _____

10. Who do you think is the greatest hockey player in Canada. _____

Week 24: Syllabication Rules 1 to 5

Objective: To teach and reinforce the first rules for syllabication

Rules:

1. A one-syllable word is never divided.
2. A compound word is divided between the words that make it.
3. When a word has a suffix, divide the word between the root word and the suffix.
4. When a word has a prefix, divide the word between the prefix and the root word.
5. When two or more consonants come between two vowels in a word, the word is usually divided between the first two consonants.

These rules should be recorded on a chart and displayed somewhere in the classroom for students use.

Day 1: Introduce syllabication rule 1 and 2. On a chart record the following words: today, turn, sidewalk, box, sunshine, hook, rainbow, cloud, sidewalk, door. Have the students say and clap each word. The students should identify one and two syllable words.

Activity Worksheet: Page 147 **A.** The students are to record the word and the number of syllables in it for each picture. **Answer Key:** Row 1: cowboy (2); sun (1); rainbow (2); moon (1) Row 2: pancake (2); popcorn (2); cake (1); star (1) **B.** The students will print each word and divide it into syllables using a hyphen. **Answer Key:** 1. in-to 2. sun-shine 3. tip-toe 4. horse-shoe 5. barn-yard 6. pan-cakes 7. rail-way 8. air-plane 9. some-thing 10. side-walk 11. foot-ball 12. wind-mill

Day 2: Record rules 3 and 4 on a chart. Read and discuss the rules with your students. Have them use a coloured marker to divide these words that are recorded on the chart with a hyphen (-). **Words:** slowly, quicker, safely, reopen, mistake, reheat, dislike, landing, softer, hardest.

Activity Worksheet: Page 148 **A.** The students will divide the words between the root word and suffix with a hypen. **Answer Key: A.** 1. small-est 2. sleep-ing 3. soft-ly 4. church-es 5. dark-er 6. fast-est 7. thank-ful 8. big-ger 9. thump-ing 10. loud-er **B.** The students will divide the words between the prefix and the root word with a hyphen. **Answer Key:** 1. re-place 2. un-fair 3. ex-press 4. dis-like 5. re-read 6. un-lock 7. dis-please 8. re-write 9. un-safe 10. un-do

Day 3: On a chart record syllabication rule # 5: When two or more consonants are found between two vowels in a word, the word is divided between the first two consonants. Under the rule record the following words: surprise, happy, children, cottage, blanket, chimney, picnic, sudden, thunder, gallop. Have the students record a hyphen between the syllables.

Activity Worksheet: Page 149 **A.** The students are to print each word on the line and divide it into syllables using a hyphen. **Answer Key:** A. for-give B. mis-take C. doc-tor D. prin-cess E. al-most F. fin-ger G. chil-dren H. can-dy I. sup-per J. fid-dle K. sud-den L. sil-ver M. num-ber N. but-ton O. gal-lop P. bot-tom Q. chim-ney R. blan-ket S. pup-py T. cir-cus U. yel-low V. bal-loon W. hun-gry X. par-ty

Day 4: Review the first five rules for dividing words into syllables. Record the following words in a list down a chart. **Words:** someone, door, sleeping, picture, unlock, run, softness, unfair, landed, finger. Have the students divide each word into syllables and record the number of the rule after it. Example: doc-tor - Rule 5

Activity Worksheet: Page 150 **A.** The students are to divide each word into syllables using a hypen on the first line and the number of syllables on the second line. **Answer Key:** 1. back-yard (2) 2. fast-er (3) 3. door-bell (2) 4. sud-den (5) 5. par-ty (5) 6. safe (1) 7. rail-road (2) 8. un-safe (4) 9. but-ter (5) 10. al-most (5) 11. mis-take (5) 12. re-read (4) 13. fox-es (3) 14. thank-ful (3) 15. stair-way (2) 16. dark-en (3) 17. dis-like (4) 18. room (1) 19. life-boat (2) 20. cloud-y (3)

Day 5: Auditory and Visual Discrimination Tests on the First Five Syllabication Rules Page 151
Auditory Test: The students are to listen carefully to each word that the teacher says. They are to circle the number of the rule they would use to divide the word into syllables. **Words:** 1. candy 2. almost 3. sidewalk 4. house 5. basket 6. riddle 7. slowly 8. rewrite 9. rainbow 10. sky **Answer Key:** 1. (5) 2. (4) 3. (2) 4. (1) 5. (5) 6. (5) 7. (3) 8. (4) 9. (2) 10. (1)
Visual Discrimination Test: The students are to record the number of syllables in each word and show how each one is divided. **Answer Key:** 1. 2, side-walk, 2 2. 2, warm-er, 3 3. 1, pen, 1 4. 2, fin-ger, 5 5. 2, sud-den, 5 6. 2, slow-ly, 3 7. 2, home-less, 3 8. 2, cur-tain, 5 9. 2 re-fresh, 4 10. 2, blan-ket, 5 11. 1 pen, 1 12. 2, mon-key, 5

SSR1142 ISBN: 9781771586887

Name: _____ Day 1 | Week 24

There are rules to follow that help you divide words into syllables. Here are two of them.

Rule 1
A word with one syllable is never divided.
bed

Rule 2
A compound word is divided between the two words.
bed - room

A. Record the word to match each picture and the number of syllables.

B. Divide the following words into syllables using a hyphen (-).

Example: for-get

1. into _____
2. sunshine _____
3. tiptoe _____
4. horseshoe _____
5. barnyard _____
6. pancakes _____
7. railway _____
8. airplane _____
9. something _____
10. sidewalk _____
11. football _____
12. windmill _____

Name: _____ Day 2 | Week 24

Here are **two** more rules to follow while dividing words into syllables.

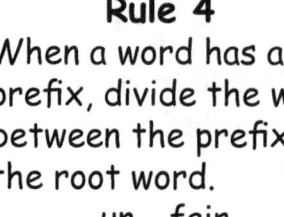

Rule 3
When a word has a suffix, you divide the word between the root word and the suffix.
rain - ing

Rule 4
When a word has a prefix, divide the word between the prefix and the root word.
un - fair

A. Divide the following words between the root word and the suffix with a hyphen (-) on the line.

1. smallest   _____   6. fastest   _____

2. sleeping   _____   7. thankful   _____

3. softly   _____   8. bigger   _____

4. churches   _____   9. thumping   _____

5. darker   _____   10. louder   _____

B. Divide the following words between the prefix and the root word with a hyphen (-) on the line.

1. replace   _____   6. unlock   _____

2. unfair   _____   7. displease _____

3. express   _____   8. rewrite   _____

4. dislike   _____   9. unsafe   _____

5. reread   _____   10. undo   _____

Name: _____   Day 3 | Week 24

Here is Rule #5 for dividing words into syllables!

Rule #5:
When two or more consonants are found between two vowels in a word, the word is divided between the first two consonants.

Examples: kid - nap   bas - ket

A. On the line, beside each word, write the word and divide it into syllables using a hyphen (-).

A. forgive _____
B. mistake _____
C. doctor _____
D. princess _____
E. almost _____
F. finger _____
G. children _____
H. candy _____
I. supper _____
J. fiddle _____
K. sudden _____
L. silver _____

M. number _____
N. button _____
O. gallop _____
P. bottom _____
Q. chimney _____
R. blanket _____
S. puppy _____
T. circus _____
U. yellow _____
V. balloon _____
W. hungry _____
X. party _____

Name: _____ Day 4 | Week 24

Syllabication Rules

1. A word with only one syllable is never divided. (house)

2. A compound word is divided between the two words. (some - thing)

3. A word with a suffix is divided between the root word and the suffix. (slow - ly)

4. A word with a prefix is divided between the prefix and the root word. (in - side)

5. A word with two or more consonants between two vowels, the word is divided between the first two consonants. (num - ber)

Use these rules while you divide the words into syllables.

A. Use the rules to help you to divide each word into syllables on the long line and record the number of the rule that you used on the short line.

1. backyard _____ ___
2. faster _____ ___
3. doorbell _____ ___
4. sudden _____ ___
5. party _____ ___
6. safe _____ ___
7. railroad _____ ___
8. unsafe _____ ___
9. butter _____ ___
10. almost _____ ___

11. mistake _____ ___
12. reread _____ ___
13. foxes _____ ___
14. thankful _____ ___
15. stairway _____ ___
16. darken _____ ___
17. dislike _____ ___
18. room _____ ___
19. lifeboat _____ ___
20. cloudy _____ ___

Name: _____   Day 5 | Week 24

Auditory and Visual Discrimination Tests on the First Five Syllabication Rules

A. **Auditory Test:**

1.	1	2	3	4	5	6.	1	2	3	4	5
2.	1	2	3	4	5	7.	1	2	3	4	5
3.	1	2	3	4	5	8.	1	2	3	4	5
4.	1	2	3	4	5	9.	1	2	3	4	5
5.	1	2	3	4	5	10.	1	2	3	4	5

B. **Visual Discrimination Test:**

Which syllabication rule would you use to divide each word into syllables? Read the word. Record the number of syllables that you hear. Divide each word into syllables using a hyphen (-). Record the number of the rule.

Word	Number of Syllables	Syllables	Rule
1. sidewalk	_____	_____	_____
2. warmer	_____	_____	_____
3. pen	_____	_____	_____
4. finger	_____	_____	_____
5. sudden	_____	_____	_____
6. slowly	_____	_____	_____
7. homeless	_____	_____	_____
8. curtain	_____	_____	_____
9. refresh	_____	_____	_____
10. blanket	_____	_____	_____
11. pen	_____	_____	_____
12. monkey	_____	_____	_____

Week 25: **Syllabication Rules 6 and 7**

Objective: Review syllabication rules 1 to 5 and to introduce syllabication rules 6 and 7.

Rule 6: When a single consonant comes between two vowels in a word, the word is usually divided after the consonant if the first vowel is short. Example: wag - on

Rule 7: When a single consonant comes between two vowels in a word, the word is usually divided before the consonant if the first vowel is long. Example: ba-by

Day 1: On a chart record the syllabication rule #6. Below the rule list the following words: dragon, magic, cabin, city, pedal, metal, petal, closet, vision, habit. Have the students put a hyphen as a marker to show where the word should be divided.

Activity Worksheet: Page 153 **A.** The students are to divide each word into syllables according to Rule #6 **Answer Key:** 1. mod-el 2. shad-ow 3. pet-al 4. drag-on 5. cas-tle 6. cam-el 7. hab-it 8. cab-in 9. mag-ic 10. fin-ish 11. clev-er 12. wag-on 13. rob-in 14. grav-el 15. liv-er 16. shad-ow 17. stat-ue 18. riv-er 19. med-al 20. sliv-er 21. met-al 22. pal-ace 23. trav-el 24. fig-ure

Day 2: Record Rule 7 on a chart with the following list of words under the rule. **Words:** lazy, baby, apron, secret, tiny, broken, bugle, zebra, evil, pilot The students are to say each word and tell where the word should be divided.

Activity Worksheet: Page 154 **A.** The students will circle the words in the box that follow Rule 7. **Answer Key:** broken, tiger, lazy, secret, pilot, icy, spider, open, obey, pupil, baby, hotel, crazy, maple **B.** The students are to record each circled word on the first line and break it into syllables on the second line. **Answer Key:** 1. broken: bro-ken 2. tiger: ti-ger 3. lazy: la-zy 4. secret: se-cret 5. pilot: pi-lot 6. icy: i-cy 7. spider: spi-der 8. open: o-pen 9. obey: o-bey 10. pupil: pu-pil 11. baby: ba-by 12. hotel: ho-tel 13. crazy: cra-zy 14. maple: ma-ple

Day 3: Review the syllabication rules 6 and 7. Have the students read the rules again. Review and practise dividing words into syllables using rules 6 and 7. **Words:** 1. dragon 2. lilac 3. clever 4. habit 5. frozen 6. music 7. figure 8. lady 9. famous 10. paper Have the students put a stroke (/) between the syllables and the number of the rule at the end of it.

Activity Worksheet: Page 155 **A.** The students will divide each word into syllables and record the number of the rule used on the lines provided. **Answer Key:** 1. ti-ger, 7 2. pu-pil, 7 3. la-zy , 7 4. cab-in, 6 5. wag-on, 6 6. pi-rate, 7 7. ba-by, 7 8. riv-er, 6 9. mag-ic, 6 10. med-al, 6 11. cra-dle, 7 12. po-ny, 7 13. cra-yon, 7 14. clev-er, 6 **B.** The students are to use the words in section A to complete the sentences. **Answer Key:** 1. baby, cradle 2. pony, wagon, cabin 3. pirate, river 4. clever, magic 5. pupil, tiger, crayon 6. lazy, medal

Day 4: Review the first seven syllabication rules with your students. On a chart list the following words down the left side: 1. magnet 2. smallest 3. goblin 4. sunshine 5. store 6. model 7. lazy The students are to divide each word into syllables and record the rule number beside each word.

Activity Worksheet: Page 156 **A.** The students are to read the rules. They are to record the number of the rule to be followed on the short line and to divide each word into syllables on the long line. **Answer Key:** 1. (2) doll-house 2. (5) hap-py 3. (4) un-fair 4. (1) house 5. (3) sweep-er 6. (5) bas-ket 7. (7) pu-pil 8. (6) wag-on 9. (5) pen-cil 10. (7) ti-ger 11. (6) rob-in 12. (5) fin-ger 13. (4) un-lock 14. (2) to-day 15. (2) pan-cake 16. (6) drag-on 17. (7) spi-der 18. (5) rid-dle

Day 5: Auditory and Visual Discrimination Test on the Syllabication Rules 1 to 7 Page 157
Auditory Test: The rules for dividing words into syllables should be posted in a place in the classroom where all the students can see and use during this part of the test. The students will read each word and circle the number of the rule that describes how to divide it into syllables. **Answer Key:** 1. (1) 2. (7) 3. (5) 4. (2) 5. (7) 6. (3) 7. (4) 8. (7)

B. Visual Discrimination Test: The students will record the rule number on the first line. They will then divide the word into syllables on the second line. **Answer Key:** 1. (2) mail-box 2. (7) ho-tel 3. (5) yel-low 4. (1) stove 5. (4) re-new 6. (3) thankful 7. (2) fire-place 8. (3) use-less 9. (5) pen-cil 10. (7) mu-sic 11. (5) pep-per 12. (2) sun-light 13. (4) un-fair 14. (7) po-lite 15. (5) thun-der 16. (6) wag-on

SSR1142 ISBN: 9781771586887 © On The Mark Press

Name: _____ Day 1 | Week 25

Read syllabication rule # 6.

Rule # 6:

When a single consonant comes between two vowels in a word, the word is usually divided after the consonant if the first vowel is short

Examples: clos - et   ped - al

A. Divide each word on the chart below into syllables using a hyphen (-).

1. model _____
2. shadow _____
3. petal _____
4. dragon _____
5. castle _____
6. camel _____
7. habit _____
8. cabin _____
9. magic _____
10. finish _____
11. clever _____
12. wagon _____

13. robin _____
14. gravel _____
15. liver _____
16. shadow _____
17. statue _____
18. river _____
19. medal _____
20. sliver _____
21. metal _____
22. palace _____
23. travel _____
24. figure _____

Name: _____   Day 2 | Week 25

Rule # 7

When a single consonant comes between two vowels in a word, it is usually divided before the consonant if the first vowel is long.

Here is another syllable rule to remember. It is #7

Examples: pi - lot   a - pron   se - cret

A. Circle the words in the box that follow this rule.

broken	stamp	tiger	kick	lazy	secret
enjoy	little	pilot	happy	icy	soap
spider	open	red	obey	pupil	funny
baby	hotel	crazy	maple	south	floor

B. Record each circled word on the lines and divide each one into syllables.

Word	Syllables	Word	Syllables
1. _____ _____		8. _____ _____	
2. _____ _____		9. _____ _____	
3. _____ _____		10. _____ _____	
4. _____ _____		11. _____ _____	
5. _____ _____		12. _____ _____	
6. _____ _____		13. _____ _____	
7. _____ _____		14. _____ _____	

Name: _____   Day 3 | Week 25

Syllable rules #6 and #7 are very helpful!

It is important to remember the rules for dividing words into syllables.

Use the rules #6 and #7 to help you to divide these words into syllables.

A. Divide each word into syllables on the long line and record the rule number on the short line.
Example: pa - per   7

1. tiger _____ ____
2. pupil _____ ____
3. lazy   _____ ____
4. cabin _____ ____
5. wagon _____ ____
6. pirate _____ ____
7. baby   _____ ____
8. river _____ ____
9. magic _____ ____
10. medal _____ ____
11. cradle _____ ____
12. pony _____ ____
13. crayon _____ ____
14. clever _____ ____

B. Use some of the words from the box to complete each sentence.

1. The _____ was asleep in its new _____.

2. The _____ pulled the _____ to an old _____.

3. The _____ sailed his ship on the large _____.

4. The _____ magician performed a wonderful _____ trick.

5. The _____ coloured the _____ using a black and orange _____.

6. The _____ boy did not run fast enough to win a _____.

Name: _____ Day 4 | Week 25

Syllabication Rules

1. A word with only one syllable is never divided. Example: boat

2. A compound word is divided between the two words. Example: cow - boy

3. A word with a suffix is divided between the root word and the suffix. Example: sail - ing

4. If a word has a prefix, the word is divided between the prefix and the root word. Example: un - fair

5. If a word has two or more consonants between two vowels, the word is divided between the first two consonants. Example: bas - ket

6. If a single consonant comes between two vowels in a word, the word is divided after the consonant if the first vowel is short. Example: rob - in

7. If a word has a single consonant between two vowels, the word is divided before the consonant if the first vowel is long. Example: pa - per

Read these syllable rules!

A. On the short line after each word, record the number of the syllable rule. On the long line divide each word into syllables.

1. dollhouse ____ _____
2. happy ____ _____
3. unfair ____ _____
4. house ____ _____
5. sweeper ____ _____
6. basket ____ _____
7. pupil ____ _____
8. wagon ____ _____
9. pencil ____ _____
10. tiger ____ _____
11. robin ____ _____
12. finger ____ _____
13. unlock ____ _____
14. today ____ _____
15. pancake ____ _____
16. dragon ____ _____
17. spider ____ _____
18. riddle ____ _____

Name: _____   Day 5 | Week 25

Auditory and Visual Discrimination Test on Syllabication Rules 1 to 7

A. Auditory Test:

1. dime	2. nature	3. rabbit	4. sunshine
1 2 3	5 6 7	3 6 5	7 5 2
5. pupil	6. darken	7. unsafe	8. paper
6 7 5	3 4 5	7 6 4	6 4 7

B. Visual Discrimination Test:

Record the rule number on the first line. Divide the words into syllables on the second line.

1. mailbox   ____ _____   9. pencil   ____ _____

2. hotel   ____ _____   10. music   ____ _____

3. yellow   ____ _____   11. pepper   ____ _____

4. stove   ____ _____   12. sunlight ____ _____

5. renew   ____ _____   13. unfair   ____ _____

6. thankful ____ _____   14. polite   ____ _____

7. fireplace ____ _____   15. thunder ____ _____

8. useless   ____ _____   16. wagon   ____ _____

Week 26: **Syllabication Rules 8, 9, 10**

Objective: To familiarize students with the syllabication rules 8, 9 and 10.

Rule 8: When a vowel is sounded alone in a word, it forms a syllable all by itself. Example: ocean: o - cean

Rule 9: When two vowels come together in a word but are heard separately, the word is divided between the two vowels. Example: lion: li - on

Rule 10: When a word ends in 'le' with a consonant ahead of it, the word is divided before the consonant. Example: circle: cir - cle

Day 1: On a chart record the following words: Canada, ocean, about, alone, icy, even, alive, open, item. Have the students say and clap each word. Have them circle the vowel in each word that is heard by itself. **Answer Key:** Canada, ocean, about, icy, open, item. Explain Rule #8 to your students.

Activity Worksheet: Page 159 **A.** The students will divide each word into syllables. **Answer Key:** 1. a-head 2. dis-o-bey 3. un-i-form 4. a-gain 5. mag-a-zine 6. zer-o 7. Can-a-da 8. a-live 9. o-pen 10. o-cean 11. a-gree 12. a-pron 13. o-pos-sum 14. o-ver 15. e-vil 16. a-lone 17. e-ven 18. un-i-corn 19. u-nit 20. zer-o

Day 2: Review syllabication rule # 8. On a chart record the following words: uniform, open, disobey, away, oval, again, gasoline, tomato, zero, ivy. Have the students divide each word into syllables

Activity Worksheet: Page 160 **A.** The students will complete each sentence with a word from the Word Box. **Answer Key:** 1. gasoline 2. uniform 3. ivy 4. opossum 5. animal 6. ocean 7. catalog 8. oboe 9. magazine 10. again 11. hero 12. obey **B.** The students are to divide the words in the Word Box into syllables on the lines. **Answer Key:** gas-o-line; un-i-form; i-vy; o-pos-sum; an-i-mal; o-cean; cat-a-log; o-boe; mag-a-zine; a-gain; her-o; o-bey

Day 3: Introduce syllabication rule # 9. On a chart record the following words: poem, violets, ruin, radio, create, giant. Have the students say, clap and locate the syllables in each word. Explain to the students rule #9: When two vowels come together in a word and are heard separately, the word is divided between the two vowels.

Activity Worksheet: Page 161 **A.** The students will divide each word into syllables.

Answer Key: 1. ra-di-o 2. di-et 3. li-on 4. ro-de-o 5. i-de-a 6. vi-o-lin 7. ru-in 8. pi-an-o 9. qui-et 10. cru-el **B.** The students will complete each sentence with a word from section A. **Answer Key:** 1. violin 2. piano 3. radio 4. diet 5. lion 6. ruin 7. rodeo 8. quiet 9. cruel 10. idea

Day 4: Introduce syllabication rule 10. On a chart, record the following words: turtle, cuddle, gentle, saddle, candle, castle, ankle, cattle, jungle, buckle. Have the students say, clap and tell you how many syllables that they hear in each word. (2) Discuss where each word would be divided into syllables. Explain Rule #10: When a word ends with 'le' and has a consonant ahead of it, the word is divided before that consonant.

Activity Worksheet: Page 162 **A.** The students will divide each word into syllables.
Answer Key: 1. ea-gle 2. nib-ble 3. an-kle 4. twin-kle 5. sad-dle 6. gob-ble 7. han-dle 8. can-dle 9. jin-gle 10. fid-dle 11. ap-ple 12. bub-ble **B.** The students will match the words from part A to the clues in part B. **Answer Key:** 1. apple 2. handle 3. candle 4. ankle 5. saddle 6. jingle 7. nibble 8. fiddle 9. gobble 10. twinkle 11. eagle 12. bubble

Day 5: Auditory and Visual Discrimination Tests on Syllabication Rules 8, 9, 10 Page 163
A. Auditory Test on Syllabication Rules 8, 9, 10: The students will circle the number of the syllable rule that suits each word said by the teacher. **Words:** 1. radio 2. lion 3. open 4. pebble 5. simple 6. violin 7. evil 8. castle 9. picnic 10. yodel **Answer Key:** 1. Rule 9 2. Rule 9 3. Rule 8 4. Rule 10 5. Rule 10 6. Rule 9 7. Rule 8 8. Rule 10 9. Rule 10 10. Rule 8

B. Visual Discrimination Test on Syllabication Rules 8, 9, 10
The students will match each word to the rule that tells how to divide it into syllables.
Answer Key: Rule 8: disobey, ocean, open, above, apron; Rule 9: giant, radio, poem, piano, violin
Rule 10: jungle, maple, pebble, needle, eagle

Name: _____ Day 1 | Week 26

Did you know that a **single letter** can be a syllable all by itself?

Read Rule 8.

When you can hear a vowel say its own sound all by itself, it becomes a syllable.

Examples: o - pen   a - lone

A. Divide each word into syllables on the line beside each one.

1. ahead _____
2. disobey _____
3. uniform _____
4. again _____
5. magazine _____
6. zero _____
7. Canada _____
8. alive _____
9. open _____
10. ocean _____

11. agree _____
12. apron _____
13. opossum _____
14. over _____
15. evil _____
16. alone _____
17. even _____
18. unicorn _____
19. unit _____
20. zero _____

Name: _____   Day 2 | Week 26

Do you remember Rule 8!

When a vowel is heard in a word, it becomes a syllable by itself

Examples: hero - her/o   ivy - i/vy

A. Use the words in the word box to complete the sentences.

Word Box					
again	ivy	hero	uniform	obey	ocean
animal	opossum	catalog	magazine	oboe	gasoline

1. Cars and trucks need _____ so they can travel on roads.
2. A police officer wears a _____ to work every day.
3. _____ is a plant that likes to grow on walls and on fences.
4. A mother _____ carries her babies on her back.
5. The tallest _____ in a zoo is the giraffe.
6. Sharks and whales live in the _____.
7. A _____ is a book filled with things that you can buy.
8. An _____ is a kind of horn that people play in a band.
9. A _____ is a book that has stories about people and places.
10. I will call him _____ on the phone.
11. The man who saved the boy from the fire was called a _____
12. Everyone in Canada should _____ their country's laws.

B. Divide the words in the Word Box into syllables.

_____   _____   _____

_____   _____   _____

_____   _____   _____

_____   _____   _____

Name: _____ Day 3 | Week 26

Here is another syllable rule to remember!

Rule 9: When two vowels are found in a word together and each one makes its own sound, you divide the words between the two vowels.

Examples: gi - ant   qui - et

A. Record each word and divide it into syllables.

1. radio _____   6. violin _____

2. diet _____   7. ruin _____

3. lion _____   8. piano _____

4. rodeo _____   9. quiet _____

5. idea _____   10. cruel _____

B. Use the words, that you had to divide into syllables, in the following sentences.

1. A _____ has strings and is played with a bow.

2. There are black and white keys on a _____.

3. We heard today's news on the _____.

4. Some people who are fat must go on a _____.

5. The _____ roared loudly and frightened the hunters.

6. A bad storm can _____ many towns and cities.

7. At a _____, cowboys try to ride bucking horses.

8. When the house was _____, the mice came out to eat.

9. Some people are _____ to animals and often hurt them.

10. My _____ to invite a clown to the party was a good one.

Name: _____   Day 4 | Week 26

Surprise! Here is Rule 10 and its the last one!

Rule 10: When a word ends in '**le**' with a consonant ahead of it, the word is divided before that consonant.

Examples: nee - dle   cir - cle   rid - dle

A. Divide each of the words below into syllables.

1. eagle _____   7. handle _____
2. nibble _____   8. candle _____
3. ankle _____   9. jingle _____
4. twinkle _____   10. fiddle _____
5. saddle _____   11. apple _____
6. gobble _____   12. bubble _____

B. Match each word from **part A** to each clue.

1. a piece of fruit _____
2. part of a door _____
3. made of wax _____
4. part of your leg _____
5. a seat on a horse _____
6. bells make this sound _____
7. to eat little pieces _____
8. looks like a violin _____
9. to eat fast _____
10. stars do it _____
11. a kind of bird _____
12. a kind of gum _____

Name: _____   Day 5 | Week 26

Auditory and Visual Discrimination Test on the Syllabication Rules 8, 9, 10

A. Auditory Test:

1. Rule 8 9 10	2. Rule 8 9 10	3. Rule 8 9 10	4. Rule 8 9 10	5. Rule 8 9 10
6. Rule 8 9 10	7. Rule 8 9 10	8. Rule 8 9 10	9. Rule 8 9 10	10. Rule 8 9 10

B. Visual Discrimination Test on the Syllaviaction Rules 8, 9, 10

Rule 8: When a vowel is heard alone in a word it makes a syllable.

Rule 9: When two vowels are together in a words and can be heard, the word is divided between the two vowels.

Rule 10: When a word ends with 'le' and has a consonant ahead of it, the word is divided before the consonant.

Words

jungle	giant	ocean	maple	radio
pebble	disobey	needle	poem	open
piano	above	violin	eagle	apple

Rule 8	Rule 9	Rule 10
_____	_____	_____
_____	_____	_____
_____	_____	_____
_____	_____	_____
_____	_____	_____

> Week 27: Review of Syllabication Rules One to Ten

Objective: To reinforce the syllabication rules and how to use them effectively.

Day 1: On a chart record the following ten words in a column down it. Have the students say and clap each word. A chart with the ten rules should be located in a visable place for student usage. Words: 1. turtle (10) 2. alive (8) 3. lemon (6) 4. expected (4) 5. pancake (2) 6. idea (9) 7. polite (7) 8. better (5) 9. sewing (8) 10. smell (1) The students are to assign the correct rule to each word.

Activity Worksheet: Page 165 **A.** The students are to read each rule and divide the words to show the syllables.

Day 2: Review the syllabication rules with the following exercise. Record the following words on a chart: painting, smell, sunset, undo, travel, uniform table, quiet, music, hungry. Have the students divide the words into syllables and record the number of the rule that they used at the end of each one.

Activity Worksheet: Page 166 **A.** The students will record the number of the syllabication rule on the short line and then divide the word into syllables on the long line. **Answer Key:** Group 1: (1) milk 2. (8) i-vy 3. (5) rib-bon 4. (6) mag-ic 5. (7) cra-dle 6. (10) rat-tle 7. (4) ex-plain 8. (2) grape-fruit 9. (3) soft-ness 10. (10) scrib-ble Group 2: 1. (2) be-low 2. (6) lem-on 3. (3) wait-ed 4. (1) smell 5. (5) sim-ple 6. (8) o-bey 7. (4) dis-like 8. (5) pic-ture 9. (9) qui-et 10. (7) pa-per

Day 3: Review dividing three syllable words into syllables. On a chart record the following words: disagree, ferryboat, applesauce, buttermilk, thunderstorm, underground. disobey, umbrella, opossums. Have the students say and clap each word. Have the students use a marker to divide the words into syllables with a line.

Activity Worksheet: Page 167 **A.** The students will complete each sentence with a three syllable word. **Answer Key:** 1. un-der-neath 2. ex-ci-ted 3. con-duct-or 4. car-pen-ter 5. en-ter-tain 6. bull-doz-er 7. skel-e-ton 8. fish-er-man 9. pro-bab-ly 10. off-i-cer

Day 4: Review the syllabication rules with this exercise. On a chart record the following words down the left side: monument, picture, smell, popcorn, polite, thistle, softness, lemon, cruel, mislead. On the right side record the numerals 1 to 10 down the page. Have the students draw lines from the word to the number of the rule they would follow in order to divide it into syllables. **Answer Key:** monument (8); picture (5) smell (1); popcorn (2); polite (7); thistle (10); softness (3); lemon (6); cruel (9); mislead (4)

Activity Worksheet: Page 168 **A.** The students will divide the underlined words in each sentence into syllables using a stroke (/) mark. **Answer Key:** 1. ba/by, rat/tle 2. gor/il/la, a/round, sad/ly 3. shop/ping, down/town, yes/ter/day 4. grand/mo/ther, arm/chair, sto/ry 5. per/form/er, tra/peze, saw/dust, be/low 6. some/times, thought/less, un/kind 7. pret/ty, blue/bird, o/ver, gar/den, look/ing 8. ap/ples, wood/en 9. cow/girl, ro/de/o, quick/ly, a/round, bar/rels 10. re/fill, bird/bath, wa/ter 11. peo/ple, hap/py, help/ing 12. wea/ther, i/deal, pic/nic

Day 5: Auditory and Visual Discrimination Test on Syllabication Rules Page 169
A. Auditory Test: The students are to circle the number of syllables heard in each word spoken by the teacher. **Words:** 1. introduce 2. fumble 3. smell 4. piano 5. football 6. cable 7. disobey 8. disturb **Answer Key:** 1. (3) 2. (2) 3. (1) 4. (3) 5. (2) 6. (2) 7. (3) 8. (2)

B. Visual Discrimination Test: The students will record each word divided into syllables using hyphens. **Answer Key:** 1. air-port 2. un-wrap 3. i-ci-cle 4. jun-gle 5. bar-rel 6. talk-ing 7. bee-hive 8. tum-ble 9. un-kind 10. ex-act-ly 11. peace-ful 12. sweet-ly 13. cre-ate 14. drum-mer 15. un-der-stand 16. dis-a-gree 17. re-fill 18. po-lite 19. ra-di-o 20. tur-tle

Name: _____   Day 1 | Week 27

There are so many rules to remember!

Read each rule carefully.

Draw lines through the words to show the syllables.

1. A word with one syllable is never divided.

    dog   coat   wood   small   fire

2. A compound word is divided between the two words.

    football   sunset   hotdog   doorway   into

3. A word that has a suffix is divided between the root word and the suffix.

    harder   looking   thankful   teacher   cleanest

4. A word that has a prefix is divided between the prefix and the root word.

    repair   disobey   midnight   unlock   submarine

5. When two or more consonants come between two vowels in a word, the word is usually divided between the first two consonants.

    letter   marble   hungry   picture   jungle

6. If a single consonant comes between two vowels in a word, the word is usually divided after the consonant if the first vowel is short.

    medal   dragon   travel   river   cabin

7. When a single consonant comes between two vowels in a word, the word is usually divided before the consonant if the first vowel is long.

    music   paper   pilot   tiger   polite

8. When a vowel is heard alone in a word, it becomes a syllable by itself.

    ivy   alarm   alive   obey   uniform

9. When two vowels come together separately, the word is divided between the two vowels.

    poem   lion   giant   violin   idea

10. When a word ends in 'le' led by another consonant, divide the word before that consonant.

    scribble   turtle   cradle   marble   bicycle

Name: _____   Day 2 | Week 27

You have learned about ten rules that you can use to divide words into syllable.

Here is a time when you can use them.

On the first line record the number of the syllable rule that you would use and then divide the word into syllables on the second line.

These rules will help me to read and spell words.

Word	Rule #	Syllables	Word	Rule #	Syllables
1. milk	___	_____	1. below	___	_____
2. ivy	___	_____	2. lemon	___	_____
3. ribbon	___	_____	3. waited	___	_____
4. magic	___	_____	4. smell	___	_____
5. cradle	___	_____	5. simple	___	_____
6. rattle	___	_____	6. obey	___	_____
7. explain	___	_____	7. dislike	___	_____
8. grapefruit	___	_____	8. picture	___	_____
9. softness	___	_____	9. quiet	___	_____
10. scribble	___	_____	10. paper	___	_____

Name: _____   Day 3 | Week 27

Some words have more than two syllables.

Did you know that there are **three** syllable words?

Examples: alphabet: al - pha - bet

unhappy: un - hap - py

A. Complete each sentence with the correct **three** syllable word.

Record it on the line in syllables in each sentence.

Example: A police officer wears a <u>un-i-form</u>.

1. The little boy was hiding _____ the bed in his bedroom.
(upon, underneath, above)

2. Joe was _____ when he saw his new bicycle.
(surprised, excited, happy)

3. The _____ led the orchestra while they played beautiful music.
(violinist, conductor, drummer)

4. The _____ fixed the broken door of the house.
(plumber, doctor, carpenter)

5. The ballet dancer loved to _____ people at the theatre.
(invite, surprise, entertain)

6. The _____ pushed the earth together and made a big hill.
(bullfighter, bully, bulldozer)

7. The _____ of a man was found in a deep hole.
(skillful, skeleton, skinny)

8. The _____ caught all kinds of fish in his big net.
(flower, different, fisherman)

9. We will _____ make your favourite cookies tonight.
(problem, probably, practise)

10. The children were rescued by a police _____.
(teacher, fireman, officer)

Name: _____ Day 4 | Week 27

Now that you know all the syllable rules, how well can you divide words into syllables?

Remember the syllable rules!

A. Read each sentence carefully. Divide the underlined words into syllables using a stroke (/) mark.
Example: re / pay

1. The baby likes to play with his blue rattle.

2. The gorilla walked around its cage sadly.

3. We rode on a bus to go shopping downtown yesterday.

4. My grandmother and I sat in a big armchair and read a story.

5. The performer on the trapeze fell into the sawdust below.

6. Sometimes Todd is thoughless and says unkind things.

7. The pretty bluebird flew all over the garden looking for a place to build its nest.

8. Put all the bad apples in the old wooden box.

9. The cowgirl in the rodeo had her horse run quickly around the barrels.

10. Please refill the birdbath with clean water.

11. People feel happy when they are helping those who need it.

12. The warm weather was ideal for a picnic at the beach.

Name: _____ | Day 5 | Week 27 |

Auditory and Visual Discrimination Test on Syllables

A. Auditory Test:

1. 1 2 3	2. 1 2 3	3. 1 2 3	4. 1 2 3
5. 1 2 3	6. 1 2 3	7. 1 2 3	8. 1 2 3

B. Visual Discrimination Test :

Record and **divide** each word into syllables using hyphens on the line.

1. airport _____
2. unwrap _____
3. icicle _____
4. jungle _____
5. barrel _____
6. talking _____
7. beehive _____
8. tumble _____
9. unkind _____
10. exactly _____

11. peaceful _____
12. sweetly _____
13. create _____
14. drummer _____
15. understand _____
16. disagree _____
17. refill _____
18. polite _____
19. radio _____
20. turtle _____

Week 28: Recognition of Contractions

Objective: To make students aware of the meanings and spellings of shortened words called Contractions.

Day 1: On a chart record the following words down the left side. **Contractions:** can't, it's, they've, we'll, isn't, haven't, doesn't. Have the students read aloud the contractions. Ask them to give the words each contraction stands for and record the words beside each one. Have them circle the letter(s) that the apostrophe stands for. **Answer Key:** 1. can't ; can not; no 2. it's; it is; i 3. they've; they have; ha 4. we'll; we will; wi 5. you're; you are; a 6. isn't; is not ; o 7. haven't; have not; o 8. doesn't; does not; o

Activity Worksheet: Page 171 **A.** The students are to record the two words that make the contractions and the letter(s) that the apostrophe is replacing on the lines. **Answer Key:** 1. is not; o 2. they will; wi 3. are not; o 4. should not; o 5. let us; u 6. was not; o 7. it is; i 8. you are; a 9. I have; ha 10. did not; o

Day 2: On a chart record the following groups of words in a column on the left side. **Words:** 1. I am 2. you will 3. could not 4. that is 5. we are 6. can not 7. that is 8. should not 9. he is 10. was not. Beside each group have a student record the contraction.

Activity Worksheet: Page 172 **A.** The students will record each contraction beside its meaning. **Answer Key: Box A:** shouldn't; he'll; aren't; don't; they'll **Box B:** can't; didn't; it's; wouldn't; weren't **Box C:** we'll wasn't; couldn't; you're; you'll **Box D:** they'll; aren't; that's; won't; don't **B.** The students will complete each sentence with the correct word. **Answer Key:** 1. couldn't 2. wasn't 3. I'm 4. it's 5. They'll

Day 3: On a chart record the following contractions: they've, we'll, doesn't, you've, didn't, I'll, haven't, weren't. Have the students read the list. Then they are to give the meaning of each contraction and locate it in the list.

Activity Worksheet: Page 173 **A.** The students will circle contractions in the Word Search. **B.** Beside each meaning the students will record the contraction. **Answer Key:** 1. couldn't 2. they'll 3. didn't 4. haven't 5. can't 6. she's 7. doesn't 8. he's 9. shouldn't 10. they've 11. there's 12. aren't 13. isn't 14. wasn't

Day 4: On a chart record the following contractions: isn't, here's, haven't, wouldn't, he's, we'll, weren't, arn't, we're. Beside each contraction have a student record the two words each one represents.

Activity Worksheet: Page 174 **A.** The students will underline each contraction in the sentences and record the meaning on the line at the end of each one. **Answer Key:** 1. we'll - we will 2. weren't - were not 3. there's - there is 4. didn't - did not 5. you'll - you will 6. wasn't - was not 7. here's - here is 8. can't - can not 9. couldn't - could not 10. it's - it is 11. there's - there is 12. you've - you have

Day 5: Auditory and Visual Discrimination Test on Contractions Page 175

A. Auditory Test: The students are to circle the contraction in each box said by the teacher. Words: 1. they'll 2. you've 3. isn't 4. wouldn't 5. didn't 6. she'll 7. we're 8. haven't 9. I've

B. Visual Discrimination Test: The students will record the contraction on the line beside its meaning. **Answer Key:** 1. they're 2. she's 3. can't 4. wasn't 5. she'll 6. aren't 7. couldn't 8. here's 9. weren't 10. I've 11. haven't 12. isn't

Name: _____   Day 1 | Week 28

A contraction is made of two words with an apostrophe

What do you know about **contractions**?

Did you know a **contraction** is a short way to write two words.

It is formed by putting **two words** together and leaving out one or two letters.

A punctuation mark called an **apostrophe** (') stands in place of the missing letter or letters.

Examples: cannot - can't   I am - I'm
we will - we'll   it is - it's

A. Record the two words that each contraction stands for and the letters that the apostrophe is replacing on the lines.

Contractions	Meanings	Missing Letters
1. isn't	_____	_____
2. they'll	_____	_____
3. aren't	_____	_____
4. shouldn't	_____	_____
5. let's	_____	_____
6. wasn't	_____	_____
7. it's	_____	_____
8. you're	_____	_____
9. I've	_____	_____
10. didn't	_____	_____

Name: _____   Day 2 | Week 28

Remember!   A contraction is made of two words.

In a contraction, an **apostrophe** (') stands for the missing letters.

Examples: you will - you'll   that is - that's

Contractions are shortened words.

A. Match the contractions in each box to the group of words that means the same. **Record** the contraction on the line beside the word group.

A. should not _____	he'll	B. can not _____	didn't
he will _____	they'll	did not _____	it's
are not _____	aren't	it is _____	wouldn't
do not _____	don't	would not _____	weren't
they will _____	shouldn't	were not _____	can't
C. we will _____	you'll	D. they will _____	aren't
was not _____	wasn't	are not _____	they'll
could not _____	we'll	that is _____	don't
you are _____	couldn't	will not _____	won't
you will _____	you're	do not _____	that's

B. Complete each sentence using one of these contactions.

(I'm   they'll   it's   wasn't   couldn't)

1. The truck _____ drive through the forest.

2. Kenny _____ afraid when he heard the loud siren.

3. _____ afraid my ship will not be able to sail under the bridge.

4. I think _____ a lovely day to go for a walk.

5. _____ use their skates at the arena.

Name: _____ Day 3 | Week 28

Let's go on a Contraction Hunt!

Remember **contractions** are words that have been shortened.

Examples: don't can't we'll

A. Look through the word search carefully and circle each contraction that you find.

```
a c g m t a u p v y w a x c y p z a x z b q c p d m n o
l b h e ' s b k c q u v b d e o r b b y c a f f e i k j
m e c f d e d i d n ' t w f q s d o e s n ' t g g h i o
o d e i f c f n r h a v e n ' t h e n h m o j e p q i r
p k n o y a k h g i j u v w r h y z i o u d f e g h n o
a n b h z n x q o b c r k s t e f u d u m i s n ' t j m
a b z y c ' d w e f o q w i o y e v h l o d z k p l m n
c i s n l t s s r g u h p x m ' n w g d n n i b j k f l
j k h w t u p v s u l t i v y l z d i n m ' x y c n d g
o i e x q p o n m i d k j x s l y a e ' o t h e y ' v e
p m ' n q v r v s t n u r t u u x z b t c b p c q s t u
y z s a b d w x a e ' f m n t h e r e ' s l k f j r i s h
g i j f c a r e n ' t l g o v w b w a c m d n e q f p g
k h l m s e u y b h i p q r x a c r w a s n ' t s t u v
n o b q r t s h e ' s j s t z y q d p e o f g n h m i j
```

B. Record the contraction in the Word Search beside its meaning.

1. could not _____
2. they will _____
3. did not   _____
4. have not   _____
5. can not   _____
6. she is   _____
7. does not   _____

8. he is   _____
9. should not _____
10. they have _____
11. there is _____
12. are not   _____
13. is not   _____
14. was not   _____

Name: _____ Day 4 | Week 28

How well do you know words called **contractions**?

Which words have the same meaning?

I know what a contraction means and can spell it correctly.

Examples: they'll - they will   haven't - have not

A. Underline the contraction in each sentence. On the line at the end of the sentence record the two words that it stands for.

1. We'll drive to the movies in our car. _____

2. We weren't invited to Tim's birthday party. _____

3. There's a big circus coming to town in July. _____

4. The car didn't stop for the red light and crashed into a truck. _____

5. You'll be the one to play the giant in the play. _____

6. Tony wasn't afraid when he heard the fire alarm go off. _____

7. Here's a big, juicy, red apple for you to eat. _____

8. You can't run in a race with a broken leg. _____

9. Billy couldn't go skating because his skates were too small. _____

10. It's a bright sunny day and we can play outside. _____

11. There's a beaver living in a dam in a pond near our house. _____

12. You've got red spots all over your face. _____

Name: _____   Day 5 | Week 28

Auditory and Visual Discrimination Test on Contractions

A. Auditory Test:

1. they've they're they'll	2. you'll you've you're	3. isn't it's it'll
4. wouldn't shouldn't couldn't	5. don't didn't doesn't	6. we'll they'll she'll
7. we'll we're weren't	8. here's haven't he's	9. I've I'd I'll

B. Visual Discrimination Test:

> can't   they're   here's   she's   she'll   isn't
> aren't   couldn't   wasn't   haven't   I've   weren't

1. they are _____
2. she is _____
3. can not _____
4. was not _____
5. she will _____
6. are not _____
7. could not _____
8. here is _____
9. were not _____
10. I have _____
11. have not _____
12. is not _____

> **Week 29:** **Antonyms**

Objective: To reinforce the recognition and usage of antonyms.

Day 1: On a chart record the two lists of words in columns on each side. **Column One:** little, awake, ugly, tall, fat, high, top, new, bright, sad. **Column Two:** happy, dull, old, bottom, thin, low, big, short, thin, beautiful. Have the students read aloud each column of words and using a marker draw lines on the chart to match the antonyms.

Activity Worksheet: Page 177 **A.** The students are to record the antonym for each word.
B. Antonyms from section A are to be used to complete the sentences.
Answer Key: A. 1. strong 2. happy 3. many 4. loose 5. under 6. old 7. big 8. awake 9. friend 10. full 11. destroy 12. swiftly **B.** 1. swiftly, slowly 2. big, little 3. sad, happy 4. over, under 5. empty, full 6. friend, enemy

Day 2: On a chart list the following words down the left side: wet, light, many, cold, weak, loose, cool, fat, large, sick. Have the students say the words in the list. Beside each word have the students print their antonyms. **Answer Key:** dry, dark, few, hot, strong, tight, warm, thin, small, healthy

Activity Worksheet: Page 178 **A. Box A:** 5, 4, 1, 3, 2 **Box B:** 4, 1, 5, 3, 2 **Box C:** 5, 4, 1, 2, 3 **Box D:** 5, 4, 1, 3, 2 **B:** 1. noisy, quiet 2. swiftly, slowly 3. hot, cold 4. over, under 5. hard, easy

Day 3: Review matching antonyms. List Group 1 words down the left side of a chart.
Group 1 Words: smile, live, high, narrow, exit, fat, first, follow Record **Group 2 Words:** lead, frown, low, enter, thin, wide, die, last. Have the students take turns locating the antonyms by drawing lines with a marker.

Activity Worksheet: Page 179: **A.** The students are to match the antonyms to the sentences.
Answer Key: 1. quiet 2. hard 3. black 4. ugly 5. laugh 6. open 7. strong 8. fix 9. late 10. different 11. answer 12. fake

Day 4: Record the following pairs of words on a chart. Have the students read the words aloud and then have them circle pairs of words that are antonyms. **Word Pairs:** 1. wet, dry 2. happy, glad 3. fat, thin 4. big, large 5. over, under 6. light, heavy 7. fix, repair 8. slowly, swiftly 9. easy, difficult 10. woods, forest

Activity Worksheet: Page 180: **A.** The students are to circle words in the Word Search that are antonyms to the words beneath the puzzle and then record them beside their antonym partners. **Answer Key:** 1. black 2. below 3. beach 4. dry 5. buy 6. warm 7. long 8. wise 9. love 10. huge 11. stay 12. listen 13. late 14. after

Day 5: Auditory and Visual Discrimination Test on Antonyms Page 181

A. Auditory Test: The teacher will say the following word pairs. If the words form a pair of antonyms the students will circle the word 'yes'. If the word pair are not antonyms the students will circle the word 'no' **Word Pairs:** 1. huge, large 2. build, destroy 3. strong weak 4. boat, ship 5. many, few 6. noisy, quiet 7. creep, crawl 8. loose, tight 9. full, empty 10. present, gift
Answer Key: 1. No 2. Yes 3. Yes 4. No 5. Yes 6. Yes 7. No 8. Yes 9. Yes 10. No

B. Visual Discrimination Test: The students are to complete each sentence with a pair of antonyms.
Answer Key: 1. asleep, awake 2. hot, cold 3. short, tall 4. win, lose 5. slowly, quickly 6. noisy, quiet 7. open, shut 8. rough, smooth 9. wide, narrow 10. throw, catch 11. smile, frown 12. straight, crooked

Name: _____   Day 1 | Week 29

Did you know that some words have **opposite** meanings? These words are called **antonyms**.

Examples: big - little;   over - under;   fast - slow

A. Match the antonyms using the words in the Word Box.

| happy | under | strong | awake | swiftly | old |
| many | friend | destroy | loose | full | big |

1. weak   _____   7. little   _____

2. sad   _____   8. asleep _____

3. few   _____   9. enemy   _____

4. tight   _____   10. empty   _____

5. over   _____   11. build   _____

6. young   _____   12. slowly _____

B. Use some of the antonyms that you matched to complete the sentences.

1. A jet flies _____ while a helicopter flies _____.

2. The _____ boy lifted the _____ girl up so she could watch the parade.

3. The girl's _____ face became a _____ one when she saw her present.

4. The billy goats walked _____ the bridge while the troll sat _____ it.

5. Please put water in the _____ jug until it is _____.

6. The fox is not a _____ to rabbits but it is an _____.

Name: _____ Day 2 | Week 29

Remember antonyms are words that have opposite meanings.

Examples: hot - cold   big - little   up - down

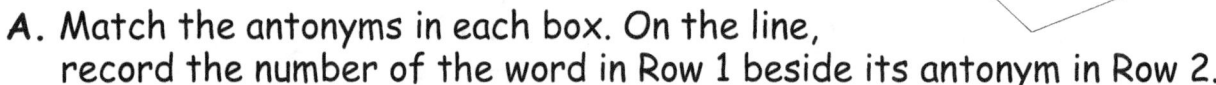

A. Match the antonyms in each box. On the line, record the number of the word in Row 1 beside its antonym in Row 2.

A.

Row 1	Row 2
1. hard	_____ lose
2. young	_____ descend
3. over	_____ soft
4. climb	_____ under
5. win	_____ old

B.

Row 1	Row 2
1. wet	_____ dark
2. many	_____ dry
3. hot	_____ weak
4. light	_____ cold
5. strong	_____ few

C.

Row 1	Row 2
1. asleep	_____ weak
2. full	_____ sad
3. friend	_____ awake
4. happy	_____ empty
5. strong	_____ enemy

D.

Row 1	Row 2
1. swiftly	_____ go
2. noisy	_____ destroy
3. easy	_____ slowly
4. build	_____ difficult
5. come	_____ quiet

B. Complete the sentences with a pair of antonyms.

1. Most cities are _____ while towns and villages are _____.

2. A bird flies _____ while a worm crawls _____.

3. The sun can be _____ while a winter wind is _____.

4. Some animals can jump _____ fences while some crawl _____ them.

5. Some tests are _____ to do while others are _____.

Name: _____ Day 3 | Week 29

Words that are **antonyms** have **opposite** meanings.

Examples: rough - smooth   scream - whisper

A. Find the words in the Word Box that match the clues. Print the words on the lines.

Word Box					
fake	answer	different	fix	laugh	open
late	strong	black	hard	ugly	quiet

1. I have five letters. I am the opposite to noisy.   _____

2. I have four letters. I am the opposite to soft.   _____

3. I have five letters. I am the opposite to white.   _____

4. I have four letters. I am the opposite to beautiful.   _____

5. I have five letters. I am the opposite to cry.   _____

6. I have four letters. I am the opposite to shut.   _____

7. I have six letters. I am the opposite to weak.   _____

8. I have three letters. I am the opposite to break.   _____

9. I have four letters. I am the opposite to early.   _____

10. I have nine letters. I am the opposite to same.   _____

11. I have six letters. I am the opposite to question.   _____

12. I have four letters. I am the opposite to real.   _____

Name: _____ Day 4 | Week 29

Let's go searching for words in the Word Search that have antonyms.

Circle each one.

Then **match** each circled word to its antonym

```
d s e i o p b r t u x v w q r s t h w a r m l p t w
e t h k j q l a y z i j a a c d g i j k l m m q s x
o a k l m m a o p q r s f t u v w x y z a b l a t e
f y g h i j c a k l m h t a e f m k i h i c d y z a
q r x o b d k e b f g h e g b i n l j g h q e f r t
b z s y t c u w v c m l r k j d o d r y c g b a w s
b e l o w n o p q r d e f s c t p n o q r d e f i x
u r c q j p k l o n g h i j k l q m p s t v u w s z
s v t k d u i m b e a c h a b d r e f n j m l o e t
o m w i j e v h w g x f y e z c s b k g u v b w x p
n p q x g h f r s x b d a b c d t u c f i e i k l m
a w b u c v d f h l o v e z m u v y v o p q h u g e
x i l i s t e n l r j s t e c d x q c b a s t a y u
```

1. white _____   8. foolish _____

2. above _____   9. hate _____

3. ocean _____   10. tiny _____

4. wet _____   11. leave _____

5. sell _____   12. speak _____

6. cool _____   13. early _____

7. short _____   14. before _____

Name: _____ | Day 5 | Week 29 |

Auditory and Visual Discrimination Test on Antonyms

A. Auditory Test

1. Yes / No	2. Yes / No	3. Yes / No	4. Yes / No	5. Yes / No
6. Yes / No	7. Yes / No	8. Yes / No	9. Yes / No	10. Yes / No

B. Visual Discrimination Test on Antonyms

Complete each sentence with a pair of antonyms found in the Word Box

```
open, shut        short, tall       straight, crooked    noisy, quiet
narrow, wide      hot, cold         smile, frown         slowly, quickly
awake, asleep     win, lose         catch, throw         smooth, rough
```

1. Children are _____ at night but _____ during the day.

2. Summers are _____ but winters are _____.

3. Some trees are _____ while others are _____.

4. I play hockey to _____ not to _____ the game.

5. A turtle walks _____ while a rabbit hops _____.

6. The _____ class soon became _____ once the teacher walked in the door.

7. Please _____ and _____ the door quietly as the baby is asleep.

8. You will have to sand the _____ wood to make it _____.

9. Some bridges over rivers are _____ while others are _____.

10. If I _____ the ball can you _____ it with your new glove.

11. People _____ when they are happy and _____ when they are angry.

12. Some lines on a page are _____ while some are _____.

Week 30: Recognizing Homonyms

Objective: To reinforce the recognition and usage of Homonyms

Day 1: On a chart list the following groups of words: to, too two; pane, pain; knows, nose; made, maid; no, know; dear, deer; hair, hare; ate, eight. Have the students say each group of words. Discuss how these words are alike in each group. (They sound the same way but are not spelt the same way and they do not have the same meanings. Discuss each pair of words. What is the same about each pair of words? (They rhyme or sound the same.) How are they different? (They have different meanings and spellings.) Explain that homonyms are words that sound the same but have different spellings and meanings.

Activity Worksheet: Page 183 **A.** The students will record the correct word beside its homonym partner. **B.** The students will complete each sentence with a homonym or a homonym pair.
Answer Key: A. 1. break 2. not 3. ring 4. bare 5. nose 6. pain 7. weight 8. steak 9. see 10. rap 11. write 12. rode **B.** 1. nose 2. stake 3 weight 4. bear, road 5. right, write 6. rode, road 7. see, sea 8. pane

Day 2: Review the meanings of homonyms with this exercise. On a chart record the following homonyms.
Words: 1. tow, toe 2. weak, week 3. some, sum 4. whole, hole 5. mail, male 6. dear, deer 7. flour, flower 8. hair, hare 9. heel, heal 10. creak, creek Which homonym means: a) the answer to a question (3. sum) b) an empty space (4. hole) c) to pull something away (1. tow) d) an animal with antlers (6. deer) e) a kind of rabbit (8. hare) f) the back part of your foot (9. heel) g) a place where fish live (10. creek) Discuss the other homonyms and their meanings in the list.

Activity Worksheet: Page 184 **A.** The students are to record the correct homonym in each sentence.
Answer Key: 1. buy 2. write 3. blew 4. hour 5. inn 6. beat 7. rode 8. dew 9. peek 10. peel 11. read 12. bee

Day 3: Review the concept of antonyms and homonyms. On a chart, record the following groups of words.
Words: 1. flower, flour 2. sale, sail 3. hate, love 4. cent, sent 5. hot, cold 6. weak, week 7. over, under 8. lost, found 9. beat, beet 10. ate, eight Have the students locate the pairs of homonyms with a red star and then locate the antonyms with a blue dot.

Activity Worksheet: Page 185 **A.** The students will classify each pair of words as antonyms or homonyms using the letters 'A' or 'H'. **Answer Key:** Group 1: H; A; A; H; H; A; H; H; A; A; H; H; A Group 2: H; H; A; H; H; A; A; H; H; A; A; H; H

Day 4: Review the meanings of antonyms and homonyms. Record the antonyms and homonym pairs on a chart. Have the students classify each pair of words as antonyms with an A and homonyms with an H.
Word Pairs: 1. cent, scent, sent (H) 2. tail, tale (H) 3. read, reed (H) 4. scream, whisper (A) 5. seam, seem (H) 6. glad, sad (A) 7. smooth, rough (A) 8. rode, road (H) 9. different, same (A) 10. reed, read (H)

Activity Worksheet: Page 186 **A.** The students will complete each sentence with the correct antonym or homonym. **Answer Key:** 1. see 2. happy 3. slowly 4. ate 5. friend 6. noisy 7. threw 8. bee 9. smoky 10. pair 11. road 12. shallow

Day 5: Auditory and Visual Discrimination Test on Antonyms and Homonyms Page 187

Auditory Test: The students will put a check mark on the line beside the type of words each pair is said by the teacher. **Words** 1. dead, alive 2. hear, here 3. love, hate 4. cool, warm 5. ant, aunt 6. bury, berry 7. wet, dry 8. made, maid **Answer Key:** 1. Antonyms 2. Homonyms 3. Antonyms 4. Antonyms 5. Homonyms 6. Homonyms 7. Antonyms 8. Homonyms

Visual Discrimunation Test: The students will select the correct antonym or homonym to complete each sentence. **Answer Key:** 1. pail 2. late 3. deep 4. creak 5. hear 6. dark 7. frown 8. scent 9. maid 10. peek

Name: _____   Day 1 | Week 30

Homonyms are words that sound the same!

Some words sound the same when they are said but are not spelled the same way and do not have the same meanings

These words are called **homonyms**.

Examples: break, brake   right, write   I, eye

A. Record each word in the Word Box beside its homonym partner.

Word Box					
break	ring	bare	nose	not	rap
weight	rode	pain	steak	write	see

1. brake   _____   7. wait   _____
2. knot   _____   8. stake   _____
3. wring   _____   9. sea   _____
4. bear   _____   10. wrap   _____
5. knows   _____   11. right   _____
6. pane   _____   12. road   _____

B. Use the correct homonym(s) to complete each sentence from the exercise.

1. Rudolph the reindeer had a big red _____.

2. We tied the wild horse to a _____ using a rope.

3. Stand on the scale so I can get your _____.

4. The cars stopped and waited for the _____ to cross the _____.

5. I use my _____ hand to _____ and eat with.

6. The riders _____ their horses on a dirt _____.

7. You can _____ ships travelling on the _____.

8. The ball hit the window and broke a _____ of glass.

Name: _____   Day 2 | Week 30

Remember: Homonyms are words that sound the same way but they have different meanings and spellings.

Examples: dew, due   fir, fur   flour, flower

There are three things to remember about homonyms

A. Record the correct homonym to complete each sentence on the line.

1. Joey went to the store to _____ some milk and bread. (buy, by)

2. At school we learn how to _____ letters and numbers. (right, write)

3. The strong wind _____ the leaves off the trees. (blew, blue)

4. The movie that we watched lasted for only an _____. (our, hour)

5. We stayed at a hotel called an _____. (in, inn)

6. My hockey team _____ all the other teams and won the big cup. (beet, beat)

7. We _____ in my father's new car to the fair. (rode, road)

8. The grass was wet with _____ this morning. (due, dew)

9. Toby tried to _____ through the hole in the fence to see his friend's new puppy. (peak, peek)

10. I helped my mother _____ the skin off the apples for an apple pie. (peel, peal)

11. Kevin _____ a story about a fox scaring a rabbit. (read, red)

12. The big _____ buzzed around the flowers in the garden. (be, bee)

Name: _____   Day 3 | Week 30

Homonyms sound the same while antonyms are opposites.

Remember!

Antonyms are words that have opposite meanings.

Homonyms are words that sound the same but have different meanings and spellings.

A. On the line record **A** if the words are antonyms and **H** if the words are homonyms in each group.

Group 1			Group 2		
maid	_____	made	blew	_____	blue
some	_____	many	buy	_____	by
true	_____	false	fat	_____	thin
nose	_____	knows	flour	_____	flower
our	_____	hour	fir	_____	fur
shut	_____	open	good	_____	bad
dear	_____	deer	large	_____	small
ate	_____	eight	heal	_____	heel
above	_____	below	hear	_____	here
love	_____	hate	rich	_____	poor
aunt	_____	ant	same	_____	different
bare	_____	bear	sea	_____	see
dull	_____	sharp	seam	_____	seem

SSR1142 ISBN: 9781771586887   185   © On The Mark Press

Name: _____ Day 4 | Week 30

Homonyms are words that sound the same but have different meanings and spellings.

Homonyms: pear, pare, pair

Antonyms are words with opposite meanings.

Antonyms: short - long;   soft - hard

Big and little are **antonyms**.
Be and bee are **homonyms**.

A. Complete each sentence with the correct **antonym** or **homonym**.

1. The doctor will _____ you in a few minutes. (sea, see)

2. The girl with a smile on her face felt very _____. (sad, happy)

3. The turtle moves _____ while walking on land. (quickly, slowly)

4. We _____ our Christmas dinner at my Grandmother's house.
    (eight, ate)

5. The coyote is not a _____ of many small animals. (enemy, friend)

6. The teacher did not like her class to be _____. (quiet, noisy)

7. Mark _____ his ball and broke a pane in the window.
    (through, threw)

8. The sting of a _____ can make some people very sick. (be, bee)

9. The sky was very _____ when the house was on fire.
    (smoky, clear)

10. We went to the store to buy me a new _____ of runners.
    (pair, pear)

11. We walked all the way to school on the dirt _____. (road, rode)

12. Some streams are _____ and you can walk across them.
    (deep, shallow)

Name: _____   Day 5 | Week 30

Auditory and Visual Discrimination Test on Antonyms and Homonyms

A. Auditory Test:

1. ___ Antonyms ___ Homonyms	2. ___ Antonyms ___ Homnyms	3. ___ Antonyms ___ Homonyms	4. ___ Antonyms ___ Homonyms
5. ___ Antonyms ___ Homonyms	6. ___ Antonyms ___ Homnyms	7. ___ Antonyms ___ Homonyms	8. ___ Antonyms ___ Homonyms

B. Visual Discrimination Test:

1. Will you please fill this _____ with grain and feed the horses.
(pale, pail)

2. If you don't hurry you will be _____ for school. (early, late)

3. A well is a _____ hole full of water in the ground. (shallow, deep)

4. The floors in an old house sometimes _____ when walked upon.
(creek, creak)

5. Did you _____ the church bell ringing during the storm. (here, hear)

6. At night we can look for stars in the _____ sky. (dark, light).

7. The angry boy had a _____ on his face. (smile, frown)

8. The _____ of flowers was everywhere in our garden. (sent, scent)

9. We asked the _____ to make our beds. (made, maid)

10. Jeff tried to _____ through a hole in the fence. (peak, peek)

Week 31: **Recognizing and Using Synonyms**

Objective: To make students aware that words that have the same or similar meanings are called synonyms.

Day 1: On a chart list the following pairs of words: begin, start; big, large; break, smash; bright, shining; cool, chilly; yell, shout; cut, slice; decide, choose. Have the students read each pair of words and tell how they are the same. (They have the same meanings.) Explain to your students that words that have almost the same meanings are called synonyms.

Activity Worksheet: Page 189 **A.** The students are to match the words in the Word Box to form a pair of synonyms on the lines. **B.** The students are to identify pairs of synonyms by recording the letter 'S' on the line. **Answer Key: A.** woods, forest; end, stop; happy, pleased; old, aged; fall, drop; part, share; fast, quick, hurt, harm; hurry, rush; scared, afraid **B.** Words that should have an S are #2, 3, 7, 9, 10, 12, 14, 16

Day 2: Review the concept of synonyms with your students using this activity. On a chart record the following words down the left side of it: beautiful, enormous, crooked, dark, cry, enjoy, fast, hurry. On the right side, in a column, record the following words: rush, like, gloomy, huge, pretty, twisted, rapid, shout. Have the students say the words in each column and then have them match the synonyms with a line.

Activity Worksheet: Page 190 **A.** The students are to match the pairs of synonyms in each box by recording the number of the word in column 1 beside its synonym in column 2 in each box. **B.** The students are to record the synonym that answers each riddle. **Answer Key: A.** Group 1: 5, 2, 4, 1, 3 Group 2: 5, 1, 4, 2, 3 Group 3: 3, 1, 4, 5, 2 **B.** 1. boat 2. beautiful 3. hear 4. woods 5. big 6. funny 7. close 8. swift

Day 3: Review synonyms with your students. Have them brainstorm for a word or words that have a similar meaning. Record these words on a chart: fast, good, fall, afraid, neat, part, begin, big, bright. Have the students brainstorm for words that have a similar meaning. Beside each word, record a word or words that are synonyms.

Activity Worksheet: Page: 191 **A.** The students are to underline words in each row that are synonyms. **Answer Key:** 1. happy, glad, pleased 2. handsome, pretty, beautiful 3. bright, shiny, gleam 4. bad, evil, mean 5. stop, end, finish 6. hurry, run, rush 7. look, see, watch 8. fat, plump chubby 9. fast, quick, swift 10. begin, start, open 11. end, stop, finish 12. tiny, small, little 13. break, smash, destroy 14. story, tale, fable 15. say, tell, speak

Day 4: Review antonyms, synonyms and homonyms with the following exercise. On a chart record the following pairs of words. **Word Pairs:** 1. amazing, wonderful (S) 2. true, false (A) 3. tale, tail (H) 4. loud, noisy (S) 5. open, close (A) 6. our, hour (H) 7. question, answer (A) 8. sleep, wake (A) 9. night, evening(S) 10. ring, wring (H) Have the students classify each pair of words as antonyms, synonyms and homonyms

Activity Worksheet: Page 192 **A.** The students are to complete each sentence with a word pair from the Word Box. **Answer Key:** 1. blew, blue 2. cried, laughed 3. open, shut 4. home, house 5. softly, loudly 6. forest, woods 7. threw, through 8. foolish, wise 9. awful, terrible 10. read, red 11. hunted, looked 12. rode, road

Day 5: Auditory and Visual Discrimination Test on Homonyms, Antonyms, and Synonyms Page 193

A. Auditory Test: The students are to circle the letter that represents the type of word pair spoken by the teacher. Listen carefully to each group of words that I say. Circle the letter A if they are antonyms, S if they are synonyms and H if they are homonyms. What are these words called? 1. narrow, wide 2. cent, sent 3. idea, plan 4. beat, beet 5. tall, short 6. looked, hunted 7. peal, peel 8. protect, guard 9. sick, healthy 10. peal, peel **Answer Key:** 1. (A) 2. (H) 3. (S) 4. (H) 5. (A.) 6. (S) 7. (H) 8. (S) 9. (A) 10. (H)

B. Visual Discrimination Test: The student will record the letter A for antonyms, S for Synonyms and H for Homonyms on the line between each pair of words. **Answer Key: Box A:** 1. (A) 2. (A) 3. (A) 4. (H) 5. (S) 6. (A) 7. (H) 8. (A) 9. (S) 10. (A) **Box B:** 1. (H) 2. (H) 3. (A) 4. (H) 5. (S) 6. (H) 7. (A) 8. (A) 9. (H) 10. (A)

Name: _____   Day 1 | Week 31

Did you know that some words have the same meaning or almost the same meaning?

These words are called **synonyms**.

Examples: funny, silly   happy, pleased   hurry, rush

A. Match the words in the Word Box to make **pairs** of synonyms. Record the synonyms on the lines.

Word Box

woods	end	forest	happy	stop
share	fall	pleased	hurry	aged
rush	old	harm	quick	drop
part	fast	scared	afraid	hurt

1. _____ _____   6. _____ _____
2. _____ _____   7. _____ _____
3. _____ _____   8. _____ _____
4. _____ _____   9. _____ _____
5. _____ _____   10. _____ _____

B. Record **S** on the line for the words that have the same meanings.

1. short   _____ long   9. looked _____ hunted
2. big   _____ large   10. shut   _____ close
3. simple _____ easy   11. hate   _____ love
4. friend _____ enemy   12. rush   _____ hurry
5. cool   _____ warm   13. our   _____ hour
6. cent   _____ scent   14. idea   _____ plan
7. display _____ show   15. high   _____ low
8. beat   _____ beet   16. quick   _____ swift

Name: _____   Day 2 | Week 31

Remember!

Synonyms are words that have the same or almost the same meaning.

Examples: big large   small little   happy jolly

A. **Match** the pairs of synonyms. **Record** the number of the word in column one **beside** its synonym in column two.

Group 1	Group 2	Group 1	Group 2	Group 1	Group 2
1. fix	___ gift	1. say	___ little	1. huge	___ crawl
2. stay	___ remain	2. glisten	___ tell	2. silent	___ large
3. told	___ lift	3. level	___ drop	3. creep	___ piece
4. raise	___ repair	4. fall	___ sparkle	4. part	___ shop
5. present	___ spoken	5. small	___ even	5. store	___ quiet

B. Read each riddle carefully. Record the word that answers each one on the line.

Answer Box

beautiful   boat   hear   woods   funny   close   swift   big

1. I have four letters. I am like a ship. _____

2. I have nine letters. I mean the same as pretty. _____

3. I have four letters. You do this with your ears. _____

4. I have five letters. I mean the same as forest. _____

5. I have three letters. I mean the same as large. _____

6. I have four letters. I mean the same as silly. _____

7. I have five letters. I mean the same as shut. _____

8. I have five letters. I mean the same as fast. _____

Name: _____   Day 3 | Week 31

There are many words that have **similar** meanings.

These words are called **synonyms**.

Examples: tired, sleepy   stop, halt   huge, enormous

A. Read each row of words carefully. **Underline** the words in each row that are **synonyms**.

1. happy	sad	glad	angry	pleased
2. handsome	ugly	pretty	thin	beautiful
3. dark	bright	poor	shiny	gleam
4. bad	good	evil	happy	mean
5. stop	stare	end	begin	finish
6. jump	hurry	walk	run	rush
7. look	hold	see	creep	watch
8. slim	tiny	fat	plump	chubby
9. fast	quick	slow	swift	dragging
10. close	begin	start	open	shine
11. end	start	stop	repeat	finish
12. lazy	tiny	helpful	small	little
13. break	fix	smash	destroy	build
14. poem	story	still	tale	fable
15. say	go	tell	show	speak

Name: _____ Day 4 | Week 31

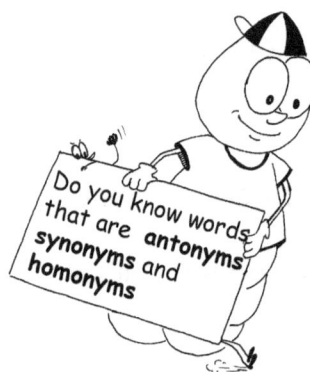

Remember!

Words may be called **antonyms**, **homonyms** or **synonyms**.

Antonyms are words that have opposite meanings.
  Example: hot - cold

Synonyms have similar meanings.
  Example: neat - tidy

Homonyms are words that sound the same but have different meanings.
  Example: weak - week

A. Complete each of the following sentences with the correct pair of **antonyms**, **synonyms** or **homonyms** found in the word box.

Word Box

house, home	laughed, cried	open, shut	foolish, wise
through, threw	blue, blew	awful, terrible	forest, woods
red, read	hunted, looked	road, rode	softly, loudly

1. The wind _____ the fluffy clouds across the _____ sky.

2. The boy _____ when he lost his book and _____ when someone found it.

3. Please remember to _____ and _____ the door quietly.

4. Their new _____ was a big white _____ that sat on a hill.

5. The teacher spoke _____ to the boys who were talking and laughing _____ during fire drill.

6. A _____ is a bigger place for wild animals to live than in a _____.

7. Jason _____ the ball that went _____ the window.

8. The _____ rabbit could not get away from the _____ owl.

9. The _____ fire left the house in a _____ mess.

10. Lisa _____ a story about a _____ fox and some rabbits.

11. We _____ and _____ everywhere for our lost dog.

12. Chris _____ his new bike on an old dirt _____.

Name: _____   Day 5 | Week 31

Auditory and Visual Discrimination Test on Homonyns, Antonyms and Synonyms

A. Auditory Test:

1. A H S	2. A H S	3. A H S	4. A H S	5. A H S
6. A H S	7. A H S	8. A H S	9. A H S	10. A H S

B. Visual Discrimination Test:

Box A			Box B		
1. short	_____	long	1. our	_____	hour
2. well	_____	ill	2. peal	_____	peel
3. smoky	_____	clear	3. tall	_____	short
4. blue	_____	blew	4. break	_____	brake
5. simple	_____	easy	5. rush	_____	hurry
6. quiet	_____	noisy	6. nose	_____	knows
7. weak	_____	week	7. hard	_____	soft
8. hate	_____	love	8. high	_____	low
9. terrible	_____	awful	9. die	_____	dye
10. foolish	_____	clever	10. above	_____	below

Phonics Information for Teachers and Parents

This information have been included to help the teacher or parent become more knowledgeable with the different aspects in the development of phonetic skills at the Grade Three level.

1. **Initial Consonant Sounds** that should be taught and reviewed are: **b, c, d, f, g, h, j, k, l, m, n, p, q, r, s, t, v, w, x, y, and z.**

    The letter 'q' is usually followed by a 'u' in words.

    The letter 'y' can be a consonant and a long and short vowel.

2. **Final Consonant sounds** are **b, d, f, g, k, l, m, n, p, r, s, t, x, y, z**

3. **Long and Short Vowels** are **a, e, i ,o, u** and sometimes **y**. Most single vowels make two sounds. Each one has a long sound and a short sound. Long vowels say their own names. Short vowels make a different sound.

    Examples of words with long vowels: long a - apron; long e: even; long i: ice; long o: open; long u: unicorn

    Examples of words with short vowels: short a - apple; short e - pen; short i - inn; short o - off; short u - cup

    Y is a vowel at the end of a word. If the word has one syllable, the 'y' makes the same sound as **long 'i'**. **Examples:** fly, sky, try

    If **Y** is the only vowel at the end of a word with more than one part, the Y usually has almost the sound of long 'e'. **Examples:** bunny, family, every

4. **Consonant Blends** consist of two or more consonants. They sound in such a way that each one is heard.

    Examples: black, train, cry, swim, spring

5. **'R' Blends** contain two or three consonants. **Examples. br, cr, dr, fr, gr, pr, tr, wr, spr, str, thr**

    Words: bread, creep, dress, frog, grain, prance, train, wrong, spring, three, street

6. **'L' Blends** contain two or three consonants. **Examples: bl, cl, gl, fl, pl, sl, spl**

    Words: black, clown, glow, plant, slide, splash

7. **Consonant Digraphs** consist of two consonants that make one sound.

   Examples: sh, ch, th, wh, ck, kn, wr

   Words: when, thin, church, sheep, pack, know, write

8. **Diphthongs** consist of two vowels blended together to form one sound.

   Examples: ou, oy, oi, ow, ew, ea, ee

9. **Soft 'C' and 'G' Sounds:** When the letters 'c' and 'g' are followed by the letters 'e, i, or y' they make a soft sound. **Examples:** mi**c**e, **c**ity, ca**g**e, **g**ym

Vowel Rules:

1. **Irregular Double Vowels** do not follow the long vowel Rule #1. **Examples:** oo, au, aw, ei **Words:** school, book, auto, yawn, eight.

2. **Short-Vowel Rule:** If a word or syllable has only one vowel and is found at the beginning or between two consonants, the vowel is usually short. **Examples:** dish, map, bug, fox

3. **Long-Vowel Rule 1:** If a word or a syllable has two vowels, the first vowel is long and the second one is silent. **Examples:** pain, white, sleep, tune

4. **Long-Vowel Rule 2:** if a word or syllable has one vowel and it is found at the end of a word or syllable the vowel is usually long.
   Examples: we, go, no, me

5. **Long-Vowel Rule 3:** If a word has two vowels together, the first one does all the talking while the second one is silent and it is usually a long vowel. **Examples:** meat, boat, feet, fair

6. **Long-Vowel Rule 4:** If a word ends with the letter 'e' and there is a vowel ahead of it in the word, the 'e' pinches that vowel to make it shout out its own long name. **Examples:** **cape, note, hide, huge**

7. **'Y' as a Vowel Rules:**

   a) When the letter 'y' is the only vowel at the end of a one syllable word, the 'y' becomes a vowel and has the long sound of 'i'.
   Examples: fry, sky, by, my

   b) When the letter 'y' is the only vowel at the end of a word with more than one syllable, it makes the same sound as the **long 'e'** vowel.
   Examples: bunny, lady, tidy, silly

Suffixes:

1. Suffixes are syllables added to the end of a root word to make a new word.
   Examples: walks, walked, walking

2. If a word with a short vowel ends with a single consonant, the consonant is doubled and then the suffix is added.
   Examples: hum - humming, run - running, bat, batted

3. If a word ends with a silent 'e', the 'e' is dropped before adding a suffix that begins with a vowel. **Examples:** like - liked, ride - riding

4. If a word ends with a 'y' preceded by a consonant, the 'y' is changed to an 'i' before adding a suffix other than 'ing.'
   Examples: try - tried, happy - happily, funny - funnier, funniest, pony - ponies

5. If a word ends with 'f' or 'fe' often the 'f' or 'fe' is changed to the letter 'v' before adding the suffix 'es'. **Examples:** leaf - leaves, knife - knives, calf, calves, shelf - shelves

Prefixes:

1. Prefixes are syllables added to the beginning of root words to make a new word. **Examples:** untie, redo, display

Kinds of Words:

1. **Compound Words** are words made of two or more words.
   Examples: housecoat, backyard, sidewalk, doorway

2. **Antonyms** are words that have opposite meanings. **Examples:** big - little, girl - boy, up - down

3. **Synonyms** are words that have the same or almost the same meaning.
   Examples: big - large, small - little, happy - jolly

4. **Homonyms** are words that sound alike but have different spellings and meanings. **Examples:** maid - made, be - bee, week, weak

5. A **contraction** is a short way to write two words. The words are written together and several letters are left out. An apostrophe (') is written to show where the letters have been left out. **Examples:** I am - I'm, can not - can't, we will - we'll

6. **A syllable** is a group of letters that may be a word or parts of a word. **Examples:** band, ban - jo, ban - a - na

7. **Nouns** are words that you can see, feel, taste, touch, smell, ride, wear and use. **Examples:** apple, table, shirt, pony, spoon

8. **Verbs** are action words. They tell how something moves, behaves, and feels. **Examples:** run, jump, crying, fights

9. **Adjectives** are words that describe how a word called a noun looks, feels, tastes. **Examples:** shiny, sour, colourful

10. **Adverbs** are words that describe how something moves. **Examples:** quickly, slowly, fast, quietly

Rules for Syllabication

Did you know: • Every syllable has one vowel sound.
• The number of syllables in a word equals the number of vowel sounds heard in it.

1. A one syllable word is never divided. **Examples:** cat, dog, tell

2. A compound word is divided between the words that make it one. **Examples:** ground - hog, up - on, side - ways

3. When a word has a suffix with a vowel sound in it, the word is divided between the base word and the suffix. **Examples:** shoot - ing, talk - ing, help - ful, hope - less

4. When a word has a prefix, the word is divided between the prefix and the base word. **Examples:** un - tie, re - pair, de - part

5. When two or more consonants come between two vowels in a word, the word is *usually* divided between the first two consonants. **Examples:** an - gry, let - ter, sud - den

6. When a single consonant comes between two vowels in a word, the word is usually divided after the consonant if the first vowel is short **Examples:** rob - in, shad - ow, wag - on

7. When a single consonant comes between two vowels in a word, the word is usually divided before the consonant if the first vowel is long. **Examples:** po - lite, li - lac, mu - sic

8. When a vowel is sounded alone in a word, it forms a syllable in itself.
   Examples: un - i - form, gas - o - line, o - pen

9. When two vowels come together in a word and are sounded separately, the word is divided between the two vowels.
   Examples: gi - ant, cru - el, po - em

10. When a word ends in '**le**' preceded by a consonant, the word is divided before the consonant.
    Examples: tur-tle, map - le, peb - ble

11. When '**be, de, ex** and **re**' are at the beginning of a word, they make a syllable of their own. **Examples:** be - came, de - fend, ex - hale

12. When a word ends in 'ed', it forms a syllable **ONLY** when preceded by '**d**' or a '**t**'. **Examples:** start - ed, found - ed

13. When '**ture**' and '**tion**' are at the end of a word, they make their own syllable. **Examples:** lo - tion, pos - ture

Teacher Record:

Development and Progress of a Student's Phonetic Skills

Name of Student: _____ Date: _____

Phonetic Skills	Teacher Comments
Initial Consonants	
Middle Consonants	
Final Consonants	
Short Vowels	
Long Vowels	
S Blends	
L Blends	
R Blends	
Final Consonant Blends	
Consonant Digraphs	
Vowel Combinations	
Singlar/ Plural Words	
Antonyms, Synonyms Homonyms	
Root Words	
Singlar/ Plural Words	

Willie Worm's Phonics Award

This award is presented to _____
for knowing the following phonics skills.

____ Initial Consonants   ____ Syllabication
____ Middle Consonants   ____ Compound Words
____ Final Consonants   ____ Antonyms
____ Long / Short Vowels   ____ Homonyms
____ S Blends   ____ Synonyms
____ L Blends   ____ Vowel Pairs
____ R Blends   ____ Word Endings
____ Digraphs